NOR:PP

QUESTION OF IDENTITY

A QUESTION OF

A play by Jack

GW00632621

CHARACTERS (in orde

Angela Fairbairn
Clare Waring . . . . *her stepdaughter*
Michael . . . . *Clare's husband*
Gyles . . . . *Angela's husband*
Kate Halloran
Det. Sgt. Baker

The action takes place in the lounge at Moat House, the family home of the Fairbairns, situated in the countryside of the Home Counties.

Time: The present

ACT I Scene 1 - Late night. Autumn

House lights and any front of curtain lighting dims to off. After a few seconds a SHOT is heard onstage followed shortly afterwards by a second SHOT, again onstage.

Curtain rises on a blacked-out stage accompanied by LOUD TICKING of a CLOCK.

After a few more seconds (and as the clock ticking diminishes to become the normal sound of a grandfather clock offstage) MOONLIGHT is slowly brought up shining in through French-windows (with curtains drawn open) towards upstage in the R wall and DULL FIRELIGHT (as from dying embers) is simultaneously slowly brought up, emanating from the fireplace in the middle of the L wall.

After another few seconds there is the sound of CAR ARRIVING (offstage R) and a BEAM (as of headlights) sweeps across the stage through the French-windows R. CAR STOPS WITH ENGINE RUNNING and then MOVES AWAY with the sound fading. A DOOR OPENS (Offstage R) followed by a door being opened in the Centre of the rear wall. The CLOCK TICKING becomes slightly louder as ANGELA FAIRBAIRN is momentarily silhouetted in the open doorway against the LIT hallway behind her.

ANGELA: *(Opening the door)* Gyles! We're here! *(Rather peevishly)* But my dear husband is not! *(She switches on the light by the door)*

GENERAL STAGE LIGHTING ON.

The Fairbairn's lounge now is revealed as a tastefully and expensively furnished room. Downstage against the R wall is a writing-bureau (or table) with a chair. The previously mentioned French-windows stand in an alcove towards Upstage in the R wall. R of the door in the rear wall is a large side table with a telephone and a tray with glasses and bottles of drink. L of the door is a smaller table with a music-centre.

There is a mirror above the mantelpiece of the fireplace in the L wall. In the hearth is a small log and a poker. Downstage of the fireplace is an easy-chair with a small coffee-table below it. There is a closed hardbacked book and an ashtray on the table. An unlit floorlamp is above the chair in the angle formed by the chimney breast and the wall.

There is a further easy-chair with a small coffee-table DRC angled towards the fireplace. Stage Centre is a settee angled slightly towards the fireplace with a small coffee table R of it.

ANGELA is in her early 30's, an attractive but rather vain and self-centred woman. She is dressed in evening-wear and carries a decorative handbag. Her love of jewellery is evident from her ear-rings and necklace and more so when she later removes her gloves to reveal a number of rings, bracelet and wristwatch.

As ANGELA moves in R she is followed by CLARE WARING. CLARE is in her early 20's, an intelligent but highly sensitive young woman whose glasses give her something of a studious air. She is also wearing evening dress, although far more discreet, under a coat. She is carrying an evening-bag and a theatre programme. She is not wearing gloves and her jewellery is far less ostentatious.

CLARE: *(As she enters)* Isn't Daddy here?

ANGELA: *(Tersely)* I should have thought that was obvious, Clare. And he promised he'd wait up.

CLARE: *(Closing the door)* His cold must have got worse and he's gone to bed.

ANGELA: *(Looking towards the French-windows as she moves towards the easy chair DRC)* I felt sure I closed those curtains before we left for the theatre. Close them, there's a dear. *(Dropping her bag down onto the chair and removing her gloves)*

CLARE: *(Momentarily annoyed before moving R, putting the programme onto the sideboard and then going to the French-windows)* Perhaps Daddy's been looking at the full moon. *(Looking out and upwards)* It isn't half as romantic, is it, when you stop to think that men have actually been up there... walked on its surface?

Clock ticking has faded away.

ANGELA: *(Breaking C)* Can't say I ever think about it. Perhaps Gyles has turned into a werewolf and gone rampaging about the countryside.

CLARE: *(Closing the curtains; smiling)* Don't be silly, Angela!

ANGELA: It was a joke, dear. And don't call me silly! I am your stepmother after all.

CLARE: I'm sorry. *(Moving to above the settee)*

ANGELA: *(Sniffing the air)* And he's been smoking!

CLARE: *(Lightly)* That's hardly a crime.

ANGELA: So much for him having a cold.

CLARE: *(Defensively)* He has got a cold. Before we left it was cough, cough, cough.

ANGELA: *(Moving back R she drops her gloves onto the easy-chair)* All the more reason for not smoking, I should have thought.

CLARE: Perhaps he had a visitor.

ANGELA: *(Removing her stole and throwing it carelessly over the back of the chair)* That's right - stick up for him. *(Shivering slightly)* It's quite cold in here. *(Looking towards the fireplace L)* No wonder - look at the fire! He could have mended it! We're not all that late.

Clock (offstage) chimes twelve.

(Looking at her wristwatch) You see... it's only midnight.

CLARE: I'll put another log on. *(Placing her bag on the L arm of the settee she starts to kneel then suddenly stops and straightens up)* It's gone! *(Looking downwards)*

ANGELA: *(Annoyed)* Don't tell me there are no logs!

CLARE: The hearthrug. It isn't here!

ANGELA: *(Moving quickly to below the settee)* We've been burgled! *(Looking all around)* But nothing else seems to be missing. *(Sharply)* Well, don't just stand there staring... put a log on the fire. *(Breaking R)*

CLARE: *(Kneeling to put log on the fire)* It's the last one.

ANGELA: *(Offhandedly)* I'll get Mickey to chop some more in the morning.

CLARE: *(Standing)* He isn't your servant.

ANGELA: Mickey likes doing things for me.

CLARE: And I wish you wouldn't call him Mickey. My husband's name is Michael.

ANGELA: My, we are touchy tonight!

CLARE: No I'm not.

ANGELA: You've been behaving like a spoilt child all evening. You've hardly said a word since we drove away from here in the car.

CLARE: *(After a moment's hesitation)* Only because I couldn't get a word in edgeways. You and Michael were...

ANGELA: Were what?

CLARE: Behaving as if the two of you were out on a date. I felt like the proverbial gooseberry.

ANGELA: That imagination of yours! You should be the writer, not Michael... at least, like Michael was!

:LARE: *(Strongly)* He still is! It's just a temporary block he's suffering from.

ANGELA: Temporary! You've both been living here for nearly three months - since soon after Kate went to Australia and he hasn't written a word. What's he doing now, anyway? You'd think he was docking the QEII - not putting his car in the garage.

The door UC opens and MICHAEL WARING enters.

Talk of the devil and he's bound to appear!

MICHAEL is in his late 20's, a good-looking man with a pleasant and easy-going manner. He is smartly dressed in a dark-coloured suit, shirt with bow-tie, with a matching handkerchief in his breast pocket.

MICHAEL: Dead on cue, apparently.

ANGELA: *(Moving to perch on the upstage arm of the chair DRC)* You've certainly taken your time.

MICHAEL: *(Closing the door)* I had a spot of bother getting the car in.

ANGELA: *(Picking up her bag to take out cigarette-case and lighter)* You don't usually have any difficulty getting it in.

Her tone of voice causes Michael to suspect a double entendre and he glances quickly towards Clare who shows no reaction.

MICHAEL: *(Moving downstage R of settee)* No, I don't, do I? Didn't seem as much room as usual.

ANGELA: *(Lighting a cigarette)* Has it shrunk? The garage, I mean.

MICHAEL: *(With another quick glance towards Clare)* I should doubt it. *(Changing the subject)* Where's Gyles?

ANGELA: *(Putting case and lighter back into her bag)* That's the 64,000 dollar question.

CLARE: I think Daddy must have gone to bed.

ANGELA: *(Coolly, blowing out smoke)* Either that or flown away on my hearthrug. It's gone missing.

MICHAEL: *(Looking)* So it has! That's odd. *(Perching on R arm of settee)* "To faraway places with strange sounding names"? The sly old fox! No wonder he didn't want to go to the theatre.

CLARE: *(Hotly)* He isn't sly! He has a bad cold.

MICHAEL: *(Easily)* I was joking, Angie.

ANGELA: *(Picking up her gloves and sitting in the chair)* Pay no attention, Michael. Your wife is in one of her moods.

CLARE: *(Tetchily)* I am not in a mood!

ANGELA: *(Off-handed)* Whatever you say, I'm not going to argue. As for being sly - aren't all men sly at one time or another? They all have something to hide.

MICHAEL: Including me?

ANGELA: Of course. *(Pertinently)* Haven't you?

MICHAEL gives a strained little laugh.

CLARE: *(Tensely)* I don't find this conversation at all funny. *(Picking up her bag off the settee-arm)* Michael and I have no secrets from each other. *(Moving above settee towards the door UC)*

MICHAEL: *(Over his shoulder)* Where are you going?

CLARE: *(Turning at the door)* Up to our room. I think I have a headache coming on. *(Opening the door she EXITS UC and closes the door behind her)*

MICHAEL: *(As he languidly slips off the arm onto the settee-seat)* Oh dear, oh dear, not another bloody headache! *(To Angela uneasily)* Just what do you think you're doing, Angela?

ANGELA: *(Coolly)* Smoking a cigarette. Do you want one?

MICHAEL: *(Rising quickly and moving L)* No, I don't... thank you. *(Bending to pick up the poker)* You know damned well what I mean... all men have something to hide! *(Stabbing at the fire with the poker)*

ANGELA: *(Stubbing out her cigarette)* Haven't you? Clare isn't pregnant, is she?

MICHAEL: *(Alarmed)* God, I hope not! I've got enough problems as it is. *(Putting the poker down and straightening up)* What made you ask?

ANGELA: She's been so unusually quiet all evening... as if there was something on her mind.

MICHAEL: *(Worried as he moves to below the settee)* You don't think she suspects anything, do you? I thought we'd been the soul of discretion.

ANGELA: *(Rising)* Would it matter? She'll have to know sometime. *(Moving to R of him)* Why not now? There's no time like the present, darling.

MICHAEL: *(Breaking to easy-chair DL)* It's too damned difficult... all living here together. Surely you can see that?

ANGELA: *(Ironically)* On top of one another, do you mean? *(Breaking DRC; with feeling)* My God, I can hardly bear him touching me any more!

MICHAEL: He still does...?

ANGELA: Occasionally. *(Lightly)* I think he must be missing Kate.

MICHAEL: *(Surprised)* Kate?

ANGELA: *(Throwing her gloves and bag onto the easy-chair)* You sound surprised?

MICHAEL: Surely you don't think...? His first wife's sister!

ANGELA: Half-sister. *(Moving URC; thoughtfully)* I don't know.... I've often wondered. *(Turning towards him)* After all, who knows what they might have got up to before I appeared on the scene... after Jenny disappeared and Kate came over from Australia to look after Clare.

MICHAEL: Not many sisters would have done that... let alone a half-sister. And you think that Gyles, suddenly lacking female companionship, might have bestowed his favours on Kate... *(flippantly)* As a token of gratitude?

ANGELA: *(Moving back DRC)* That hardly sounds like Gyles!

MICHAEL: *(Moving to squat on L arm of settee)* To be fair he has been more than generous... having me and Clare living here.

ANGELA: *(Offhandedly)* He can afford it. Although I was rather surprised when he invited you both.

MICHAEL: Well, as he put it, he thought a change of scene might get my creative juices flowing again. *(Depressed)* I'm beginning to think they've dried up for good! *(After a brief pause)* But why were you surprised? I am his son-in-law... she's his daughter.

ANGELA: *(Moving her bag and gloves to allow her to sit)* It's not as if he's ever shown any real affection for Clare. Not what you'd expect from a father. Oh, in her eyes he can do no wrong. She obviously loves him deeply. But he never seems able to really make contact with her... certainly not physical contact. It's as though he can't bring himself to touch her.

MICHAEL: Why do you think that is?

ANGELA: I don't really know. From what he's told me, Clare is the absolute image of her mother when Jenny was her age.

MICHAEL: Surely that fact alone would make her something special for him?

ANGELA: *(Thoughtfully as she rises and moves DC)* You would think so, wouldn't you? But, at times, it almost seems to have the reverse effect... as if he resented her. Sometimes I've even thought that he looks guilty.

MICHAEL: Of what? There was nothing suspicious about her mother's disappearance, was there?

ANGELA: Not so far as I know. Apparently one day she just wasn't here any more... vanished without trace! Disappeared into thin air!

MICHAEL: Leaving a young child - no more than a baby in arms - behind her. Most unusual!

ANGELA: *(Breaking R)* If only he would disappear as easily!

MICHAEL: *(Lightly)* Perhaps he has... *(looking down at the hearth)* on his magic carpet!

ANGELA: What can have happened to it? I suppose in one of your crime novels it would have been bloodstained and disposed of along with the corpse?

MICHAEL: I hope I can be less hackneyed than that. *(Depressed again)* At least I used to be!

ANGELA: For God's sake, stop being so morose and sorry for yourself, Mickey.

MICHAEL: *(Rising quickly)* It's all right for you... you don't know what it feels like! Not being able to write... wondering whether I shall ever write again. *(Staring moodily into the mirror over the mantelpiece)* I can't even stand looking at myself! *(Turning angrily away)*

ANGELA: *(Moving to below settee)* You've got to give yourself time.

MICHAEL: *(Savagely)* Time! I haven't got time! I've given myself time... taken advantage of Gyles' hospitality...

ANGELA: It pleases him to appear magnanimous... Lord of the manor... patron of the arts.

MICHAEL: And in return what have I done?

ANGELA: Taken advantage of his wife? I haven't noticed you being too reluctant.

MICHAEL: I do have some feelings... better instincts.

ANGELA: *(Moving to R of him)* Darling, it's not your better instincts that interest me! *(Winding her hands and arms around him)*

MICHAEL: *(Worried)* He might come in!

ANGELA: He'll be sound asleep... snoring. My God, how he snores! Like a machine-gun. *(Pulling him towards her face with a hand at the back of his head)*

MICHAEL: But Clare...

ANGELA: She's upstairs sulking. *(Her mouth closes on his and she kisses him hungrily. MICHAEL responds before suddenly pushing her away)*

MICHAEL: *(Urgently as he looks quickly towards the door)* I think someone's coming!

To his dismay ANGELA snatches another brief kiss before coolly moving away towards the easy-chair DRC as the door opens and GYLES FAIRBAIRN ENTERS UC. GYLES is in his mid-40's. He is wearing a silk dressing-gown over pyjamas and with a pair of leather slippers on otherwise bare feet.

(With strained affability) Well, well, if it isn't the man who came back!

GYLES: *(Sharply; in open doorway)* What!?

ANGELA: Pay no attention, Gyles. I was about to come and see if you were all right.

GYLES: *(Closing the door)* Why shouldn't I be? *(Moving DC)*

ANGELA: Your cold.

GYLES: Oh, that! Much better, thanks.

MICHAEL: You sound more like yourself.

GYLES: *(Joking)* I could hardly be anyone else, could I?

MICHAEL: All that coughing you were doing.

ANGELA: You said you'd wait up. *(Sitting in easy-chair DRC)*

GYLES: So I have. Thought I'd have a good long soak in a hot tub. Seems to have worked wonders - made a new man of me! *(Suddenly coughs)* Well almost! Did you enjoy the show? Where's Clare?

MICHAEL: *(Starting to reply)* Upstairs. She has....

ANGELA: *(Interrupting sharply)* What has happened to the rug? The one that Michael should be standing on - but isn't?

GYLES: Oh, yes, the hearthrug. The thing is... I spilled some wine on it... can't think quite how it happened... must have dozed off with the glass in my hand. I was sitting in that chair. *(Indicating the chair DL)*

ANGELA: *(Rising quickly; annoyed)* Gyles, how could you!

GYLES: I'm sorry. I fancied something a bit sharp... for my throat. So I had a glass of red.

ANGELA: But you never drink red... you've always said it tastes like... well, you know very well what.

MICHAEL: At least you chose the right colour. *(GYLES looks mystified)* For blood!

GYLES: Why do you say that?

MICHAEL: I didn't - it was Angela. She said that if this was in one of my books, the reason for the rug having disappeared would be because it was bloodstained.

GYLES: *(With a slightly nervous smile)* Oh, I see. Well, it hasn't exactly disappeared. It's down in the cellar drying next to the boiler-fire.

ANGELA: It's ruined, isn't it?

GYLES: No, of course not. I gave that end *(pointing to the downstage end of the hearth)* a good scrub... found some stuff in the kitchen.

MICHAEL: *(Jokingly)* Sounds like a TV commercial!

ANGELA: *(Sharply)* How could you be so careless?

GYLES: It was an accident.

ANGELA: *(Persisting)* After all that fuss we had getting it through the Customs, coming back from that Mediterranean cruise. Where was it you bought it for me... Algiers or Casablanca?

GYLES: *(Hesitating)* Algiers.

MICHAEL: No, it was Casablanca, Gyles. *(To Angela)* I remember you telling me you'd been looking for Rick's Bar.

ANGELA: That's right. I so wanted to go in and say "Play it again, Sam". *(To Gyles)* If that rug is spoilt...

GYLES: *(Touchily)* I've told you it isn't! *(Sitting R end of the settee)*

MICHAEL: *(With mock solemnity)* It's a serious offence... tampering with the evidence at the scene of a murder - and where's the body?

ANGELA: *(As Gyles reacts)* You'd better drop it, Michael. Gyles is obviously not amused.

MICHAEL: *(Apologetically)* Sorry! *(Moving to the chair DL; conversationally)* So how was your evening? I see you've been reading one of my books. Which one? *(Picking up the book from the coffee-table as GYLES hesitates)* "Model For Murder", my latest - or should I say last... Inspector Dunne's last case! *(Putting the book down and sitting in the chair)* What did you think? *(Quickly)* No, don't tell me, I might get depressed and Angela doesn't like me to be depressed. Do you, Angela?

ANGELA does not reply and there is a brief pause.

(Brusquely; as he rises) Well, I feel like a drink. May I, Gyles? *(No reply)* Gyles!

GYLES: *(Becoming aware he is being addressed)* What?

MICHAEL: I asked if you minded me having a drink?

ANGELA: *(Shortly)* You know he doesn't - he's said so often enough.

MICHAEL: *(Moving up L of settee and above it to the sideboard UR)* Thanks all the same. Anyone join me?

ANGELA: *(As GYLES shakes his head)* Please. The usual.

MICHAEL: *(Pouring drinks)* One good old usual coming up.

The door opens and CLARE ENTERS UC, now without her coat and handbag.

Just in time! Fancy a drink? It might do you good.

CLARE: *(Closing the door)* No, thanks. I should have thought you'd had more than sufficient this evening... at the bar beforehand and the interval. *(Moving L of the settee to the fireplace)*

MICHAEL: That's what I like about the theatre... if the play's no good, there's always the interval - or better still, two intervals!

CLARE: I thought the play was very good. *(To Gyles)* I'm sure you would have liked it, Daddy. Is that stupid cold any better?

GYLES: Yes, quite a lot. *(Coughs)* Well, quite a bit.

CLARE: *(As MICHAEL moves downstage with two glasses)* What's happened to the rug?

GYLES: *(As Michael hands a glass to Angela)* A small accident. I spilt some wine. It's in the cellar drying. Angela's annoyed with me.

CLARE: Some people are easily upset.

ANGELA: *(To Michael)* Listen who's talking! *(They both drink)*

GYLES: *(To Clare)* Tell me about the play. See, what was it again?

CLARE: Daddy! You can't have forgotten... Shakespeare's "Comedy of Errors". Where did I put the programme? *(Seeing it on the sideboard she moves to fetch it, hands it to him over the back of the settee and then continues her move to sit in chair DL)* It's about these two pairs of identical twin brothers... Dromio and Antipholus of Ephesus and Dromio and Antipholus of Syracuse.

GYLES: *(Looking at the programme without real interest)* Sounds complicated.

CLARE: Of course the two pairs of twins weren't identical, on stage I mean.

MICHAEL: Darling, how many theatrical companies do you think can come up with one pair of identical twins... let alone two? It's called 'the suspension of disbelief'... by the audience that is.

CLARE: *(Astringently)* I didn't know you were so well informed.

MICHAEL: *(Unperturbed)* Just goes to show you don't know everything about me. Then, how many of us do know everything about another person, eh, Gyles?

GYLES: Fortunately, perhaps.

MICHAEL: *(Taking Angela's empty glass)* Another?

ANGELA: I'd better not or I may have to get up in the night.

MICHAEL: *(Moving up to the sideboard)* I think I'll risk it.

CLARE: Michael, please!

MICHAEL: For heaven's sake relax! I don't remember driving back without due care. Didn't hit the odd pedestrian... not even a froggy who would a-wooing go. If I had, let's hope for his sake it would have been on the return trip! *(Pouring himself another drink)*

CLARE: *(Coldly)* Was that supposed to be funny?

MICHAEL: Yes. Wasn't it?

CLARE: Not very.

ANGELA: *(To Michael)* You know Clare can't stand anything the least bit suggestive. She's so prudish. *(Looking at Gyles)* Must take after her mother.

GYLES looks towards Angela and then Clare.

CLARE: *(Rising quickly)* I am not prudish! And leave my mother out of this. *(GYLES continues to look fixedly at her; to him)* What's the matter? *(Moving to look in the mirror over the fireplace)* Is it my hair or my lipstick?

GYLES: *(Vaguely)* No, it's nothing.

CLARE: *(Turning to him)* But you were looking at me so oddly... almost as if you'd never seen me before.

GYLES: I'm sorry, I didn't mean to upset you.

MICHAEL: *(To CLARE, as he moves DRC)* I think you're overtired. Why don't you go to bed?

CLARE: *(Sharply)* I'll go to bed when I'm good and ready! *(MICHAEL gives a careless shrug and drinks)*

GYLES: *(To Clare)* You're so very like your mother.

ANGELA: *(Sarcastically)* Now there's an original thought!

CLARE: *(Neurotically)* My mother is dead! Must we talk about her?

MICHAEL: *(Sympathetically)* You don't really know that.

CLARE: *(Losing control)* She is, I know she is! She'll never come back... never! *(Regaining her composure)* I better had go to bed. I'd almost forgotten it's tomorrow that Aunty Kate gets back. *(Gyles reacts)* I have to be up early to drive to the airport. *(She bends towards Gyles to pick up the programme from the settee)* Goodnight, Daddy, I'm sorry I got upset.

GYLES: Don't worry about it. *(Kissing her cheek)* Goodnight, Clare.

CLARE straightens up quickly, obviously taken by surprise. One hand moves involuntarily to gently touch her cheek. ANGELA and MICHAEL exchange surprised looks.

CLARE: *(Moving above the settee; to Michael)* Are you coming?

MICHAEL: *(Indicating his glass)* When I've finished this.

CLARE: Goodnight Angela.

ANGELA: *(Rising)* I'll come up with you and take a quick shower. *(Picking up her bag and gloves. MICHAEL steps aside R and hands her the stole off the chair-back)* Thanks, Michael.

MICHAEL: You're welcome.

ANGELA 'rewards' him with a smile and starts to move R of the settee towards the door. CLARE opens the door for ANGELA to pass her.

ANGELA: After you... beauty before age! *(CLARE does not respond and EXITS UC; ANGELA turns at the open door)* Now you two can share all your male secrets! *(EXITS UC closing the door behind her)*

MICHAEL: *(Draining his glass and taking it to the sideboard UR)* Don't know that I have any. How about you, Gyles?

GYLES: *(Rising and breaking DL)* None that I can think of.

MICHAEL: Really? I am surprised.

GYLES: *(Without turning to him; tensely)* What do you mean?

MICHAEL: *(Moving DC)* Oh, I think you know. Still, none of my business, is it?

GYLES: *(Sitting in chair DL)* I haven't the vaguest idea what you're talking about.

MICHAEL: *(Deviously)* No, of course you haven't. *(Moving to the fireplace)* Looks as if we're out of logs. I'll have a go at cutting some in the morning, if you don't feel up to it.

GYLES: Thanks.

MICHAEL: *(Moving to sit R end of the settee)* Only too pleased to make myself useful. I'm sure I've mentioned it before, but I really do appreciate you and Angela having us here. You must have thought that when she got married you'd got Clare off your hands.

GYLES: What's that saying? Not so much losing a daughter as gaining a son. A well known writer at that. Still no stirring of the creative urge? Not that I'm trying to get rid of you, of course.

MICHAEL: Occasionally I get a glimmering of an idea, but somehow I seem totally incapable of reaching out and taking a firm hold of it. It's like a mirage in the desert... one minute it's there and you'd swear it was for real... and the next... gone with the wind!

GYLES: Worrying about it can't help.

MICHAEL: You're right, but unfortunately, I can't help worrying. After all, I do have a wife to support... hopefully in the manner that you brought her up.

GYLES: I'd say you haven't done too badly so far.

MICHAEL: No, but this situation does seem to be getting on her nerves. I'm hoping she'll be better when Kate gets back tomorrow. Give her something to think about. I suppose you must have been missing her too?

GYLES: *(Rising and crossing downstage to DRC)* Yes... yes, of course. It's been... how long now?

MICHAEL: About three months, I believe. It must have been great seeing her family and friends in Australia after all the years she'd been with you since Clare's mother disappeared.

GYLES: *(Tautly, as he moves towards the french-windows R)* Yes, yes, it must have been.

MICHAEL: *(Apologetically)* Sorry! It still distresses you, doesn't it? Let's change the subject. You can tell me now that Angela's not here.

GYLES: *(Turning)* Tell you what?

MICHAEL: *(Rising and moving to the fireplace)* Come on, we're both men of the world.

GYLES: What's that supposed to mean? *(Sharply)* If you've got something to say... for God's sake say it!

MICHAEL: Before you came down I jokingly accused you of being a sly old fox. Clare objected.

GYLES: *(Shortly)* That was good of her.

MICHAEL: You certainly fooled me.

GYLES: *(Apprehensively)* About what?

MICHAEL: Relax Gyles, your deep dark secret is safe with me. I shan't tell a living soul, I promise. Scout's honour!

GYLES: *(Moving to DC)* I wish I knew what the devil you're talking about.

MICHAEL: I'm talking about your pretence of being stricken down by a cold as an excuse for not going to the theatre.

GYLES: Why should I need an excuse? If I didn't want to go I could have just said so.

MICHAEL: After Angela had bought you a ticket? That certainly would have aroused her suspicions.

GYLES: Suspicions! What about?

MICHAEL: Look, it's alright. I'm a married man myself but without having served such a long sentence. By the way, is it true one gets time off for good behaviour? *(GYLES reacts impatiently)* O.K. so you had other plans for this evening?

GYLES: *(Annoyed)* Damn it, Michael! What other plans?

MICHAEL: While the cat's away... *(GYLES steps forward threateningly)* You're right, your extra-marital activities are none of my business. I'm just surprised that's all. I had no idea.

GYLES: And neither have I... not the least idea what you're talking about.

MICHAEL: Come of it, Gyles! Off the record... between the two of us... man to man... who's the lucky lady? One of the barmaids at "The Crown" in the village I'd guess - the blonde or the redhead? If she really is a redhead. I'd say the blonde. Gentlemen do prefer blondes, don't they? What's her name?

GYLES: I've no idea.

MICHAEL: I've seen you chatting her up often enough - when Angela wasn't there, of course - as well as looking down her... that cleavage must be worth a good few extra pints a night when she's on duty. Her evening off was it?

GYLES: *(Breaking towards DR)* How should I know?

MICHAEL: *(Suddenly)* That's it - Babs. The three 'B's... blonde, busty and beddable! How was she?

GYLES: You really are letting that creative imagination of yours run away with you. I've been here all evening.

MICHAEL: *(Moving L of settee to above it)* That won't wash, old sport. You've been out in your car. And that is fact, not fiction. *(GYLES registers alarm)* When I drove out of the garage to go to the theatre your car was in its usual position and reversed in. When we came back I had difficulty getting in - you'd hardly left me enough room. And you'd driven straight in without reversing. What was the matter? Were you in a hurry? Had Babs' charms - hidden or otherwise - made you lose all track of time?

GYLES: *(Tautly)* Have you quite finished?

MICHAEL: *(Continuing his move R of settee to DC)* No, not quite. There were faint damp tracks on the garage-floor and your tyres showed definite traces of mud. Now, there's been no rain for days - hardly any to speak of for weeks. One of the driest summers on record... hosepipe bans, reservoirs half empty or half full if you're more of an optimist... standpipes being got ready...

GYLES: I suppose all this comes of your writing crime novels. You really should have been a detective.

MICHAEL: No thanks, not my cup of tea... but some of it does rub off.

GYLES: *(Crossing below him to DLC)* So what do you deduce from your detailed observations, Holmes?

MICHAEL: *(Breaking R)* Elementary, my dear Watson, you do admit that you went out?

GYLES: There seems no point in trying to deny it any longer. I've been caught red-handed - or rather muddy-tracked. *(Sitting chair DL)* But at least you can understand my motive.

MICHAEL: Of course, and don't worry. Your secret is safe with me. I dropped Angela and Clare at the front door before driving round to the garage. *(Sitting chair DR)* So I'd say that you picked up the bustiful Babs at some quiet location...

GYLES: That I don't admit.

MICHAEL: Or whoever the lady was. Let's call her Madame X. And you drove to some secluded lovers' lane - not too far away, as time was all important. Somewhere low-lying and obviously quite damp. Perhaps made muddy by farm tractors. One of those sunken lanes with a nearby spring. How am I doing so far?

GYLES: You should make Superintendent before too long.

MICHAEL: Thanks. One thing I don't understand is why tonight? You knew Angela had got tickets for the theatre, so why go through that rigmarole of having a cold? Were you that desperate to see her?

GYLES: It seemed too good an opportunity to miss. As you said, while the cat's away...!

MICHAEL: Yes, I didn't think of that. Perhaps I shan't make Super quite so soon after all. *(Rising)* However, there is just one thing more...

GYLES: *(Apprehensively)* What's that?

MICHAEL: *(Smiling)* I hope it was worth it!?

GYLES: *(Relaxing)* No comment!

Both laugh as the door opens and ANGELA ENTERS UC, now in a dressing-gown and slippers.

ANGELA: *(As she enters)* It sounds as if that was a good one. Was it the one about the vicar and the barmaid? *(ANGELA is closing the door and misses the interchange of looks between the two men)*

MICHAEL: *(Teasingly)* Wouldn't you like to know? That didn't take you long.

ANGELA: *(Moving downstage R of settee)* I wondered what I was missing. *(Looking towards Gyles)*

GYLES: As Michael said - wouldn't you like to know?

ANGELA: *(Sitting R end of settee)* Yes, I should. *(Looking from one to the other)* But I can see that I shan't.

MICHAEL: *(With appropriate hand movements)* Hear no evil, speak no evil, see no evil, eh, Gyles?

GYLES: *(Rising)* I think I'll make that my exit line and go to bed.

ANGELA: Running scared? I'll be up in a while. After that shower I feel like a nightcap.

GYLES: *(Moving L of settee)* What would you like? *(Continuing his move above settee)*

ANGELA: Michael will get it. He knows what I like. *(With a sideways glance towards Michael)*

GYLES: *(Hovering hesitantly URC)* I, er... I thought I'd sleep in the spare room tonight.

ANGELA: *(Not displeased)* As you wish. Why?

GYLES: Oh, this cold. I'd hate to pass it on. *(Glancing conspiratorially towards Michael)*

ANGELA: It seems so much better.

GYLES: *(Clearing his throat)* Yes, it is but no doubt the germs will be lingering on.

MICHAEL: *(Quizzically)* Like the memory?

ANGELA: In that case, I'll say goodnight.

GYLES: Yes, goodnight. *(Hesitating as if unsure whether or not to kiss her)* Goodnight, Michael. *(Moving to the door)*

MICHAEL: Goodnight, Gyles. *(Feigning)* Too bad you couldn't be with us this evening. Hope you'll feel better after a good night's sleep.

GYLES: Thanks. Goodnight. *(Exits UC, closing the door behind him)*

ANGELA: *(Expressing surprise)* Well, what do you make of that?

MICHAEL: I thought it was very considerate of him. Don't tell me you're not pleased?

ANGELA: On the contrary, it's so unusual, that's all. Quite out of character. Not like Gyles in the least. Do I get my nightcap or not?

MICHAEL: *(Moving up to the sideboard UR)* Perhaps he's been overdoing things - needs a good rest. *(Pouring drink)*

ANGELA: Too bad your dear little wife is here. It would have been an ideal opportunity, wouldn't it? *(Michael moves to R of settee with glass)* Not joining me?

MICHAEL: I'd better not.

ANGELA: *(Taking the glass)* Worried what darling Clare might say? *(Drinks)*

MICHAEL: She'll be asleep. *(Breaking DR)* One thing's for sure... she won't be waiting for me with open arms.

ANGELA: *(Toasting)* To married life... with the right person! *(Thoughtfully)* If only Gyles could be made to disappear.

MICHAEL: *(Treating it as a joke)* On his flying carpet? I'm certainly no Houdini.

ANGELA: *(Pointedly)* But you do write murder stories.

MICHAEL: Or did! *(Suddenly looking keenly at her)* You're not serious!?

ANGELA: *(Drinks; after a pause)* Of course not. *(Laughing)* You should have seen the look on your face!

MICHAEL: Murderers usually get found out. Always when my Inspector Dunne is on the case.

ANGELA: *(Mockingly)* He always gets his man? *(Holding her empty glass out towards him)*

MICHAEL: *(Moving to take it)* Or woman. *(Lifting the glass)* Another?

ANGELA: No, thanks.

MICHAEL: *(Taking the glass to the sideboard UR)* I should be going up. If Clare's going to be off at God knows what hour she's bound to wake me up.

ANGELA: Must you? It's not often that we get the chance to be alone - with Kate back it will be even worse.

MICHAEL: Beats me why she's coming back... why she's stayed on here all these years. Particularly after we got married and Clare moved away.

ANGELA: That's occurred to me more than once but I've got so used to her being here - almost like a ménage à trois!

MICHAEL: *(Moving DRC)* You'd think she'd want to start a life of her own... having spent all those years bringing up Clare.

ANGELA: She's like a mother to her. *(Rising)* And the way she looks at me sometimes... as if somehow I had been to blame for her sister's disappearance.

MICHAEL: But you never even knew her, did you?

ANGELA: No. But it's as though she resents me for having taken Jenny's place... as though she feels that she has more right to it than I have.

MICHAEL: *(Surprised)* As Gyles' wife?

ANGELA: Why not? If I was out of the way there'd be no need for her to look for a life of her own. She'd already have a family ready-made - husband, daughter and son-in-law!

MICHAEL: Gyles might have other ideas.

ANGELA: It's an interesting possibility though, isn't it? For us. Of course there would still be the question of what to do about Clare? *(Seductively)* Do you still feel like going up to bed?

MICHAEL: *(Moving to her below the settee)* On second thoughts... the settee will do! *(MICHAEL takes her in his arms and draws ANGELA down with him onto the settee and they kiss passionately. Removing his arms from around her MICHAEL commences to ease himself out of his jacket)*

CURTAIN

ACT I Scene 2

Next morning. At rise: The stage is empty. The french-windows R stand open with BRIGHT SUNLIGHT entering through them. The sound of BIRDSONG is heard (off R) The door UC is ajar. There is no fire in the grate L.

After a few seconds GYLES ENTERS through the french-windows R. He is wearing a crew-neck sweater, slacks and shoes. He appears purposeful as he crosses to the door, looks quickly out into the hallway, closes the door and moves down to the bureau/writing table DR. Pulling out its chair he sits and begins to search the bureau's contents and drawers.

Absorbed in examining the contents he is not aware as the door opens and ANGELA ENTERS UC. She is wearing a summer frock and sandal-type shoes and is carrying a folded-up newspaper and three or so envelopes.

Birdsong fades to off.

ANGELA: *(In the open doorway)* Looking for something?

GYLES: *(Startled; as he closes a drawer)* What? *(Half-turning)* Oh, no, nothing in particular. I really must get around to clearing this out sometime.

ANGELA: *(Closing the door)* I've suggested that often enough, haven't I? *(Casually)* Did you sleep well?

GYLES: Yes thanks, did you?

ANGELA: Surprisingly well. I hadn't realised I was quite so tired.

GYLES: *(Rising and pushing in the chair)* You'd had a long day. Is that the morning paper?

ANGELA: *(Moving DC)* Yes and the post has just been. Probably more bills. *(Handing Gyles the newspaper as he moves below the easy-chair to her)* Which reminds me, have you written a cheque for the electricity? The bill's in there. *(Indicating the bureau as she sits R end of settee)* We don't want it cutting off with a freezer full of food.

GYLES: *(Sitting in the easy-chair and opening the newspaper)* I'll... *(briefly hesitating)* see to it later.

ANGELA: *(Proceeding to open the envelopes)* Don't forget! Have you had breakfast?

GYLES: I had a bite with Michael. He's quite a good cook.

ANGELA: I should have thought you knew that already.

GYLES: I do. I was passing a remark, that's all. Clare's a very lucky young woman.

ANGELA: *(Half to herself)* Isn't she just! *(To Gyles)* Where is Michael?

GYLES: He went out to chop some logs. Only wish I had his energy. The time he's been gone, he must be felling a tree.

ANGELA: *(Without interest)* I suppose Clare got off all right?

GYLES: Yes. Didn't you hear the car?

ANGELA: *(Curtly)* If I had I shouldn't have asked. I thought you slept well?

GYLES: I did... considering the strange bed.

ANGELA: *(Reading the contents of an envelope)* That was your choice. At least your cold seems to have disappeared.

GYLES: Must have been one of those twenty-four hour summer-flu bugs. Probably all this dry weather. I'm just reading this is one of the longest droughts within living memory.

ANGELA: *(Still reading; disinterested)* Really. If you're dead I don't suppose it matters. *(Carelessly dropping a couple or so envelopes and contents onto the coffee-table to R of her)* More junk mail! Save the Children, or the Whales or what-have-you and the Reader's Digest notifying that we shall be receiving Prize Draw documents in the near future. Why don't they just send them? This is from Babs.

GYLES: *(Alert)* Babs?

ANGELA: Barbara Dawson. You must remember them, Gyles... Barbara and Francis - or was it Frank? We met them in the Canaries. Or was it the Bahamas? No matter. Barbara's asking us over next weekend. Won't that be nice?

GYLES: *(Uncomfortably)* Surely we can't go.

ANGELA: Why on earth not?

GYLES: Well... with Clare and Michael here. And Kate coming back today. It wouldn't be very polite.

ANGELA: *(Petulantly)* No, I suppose not. *(Putting the letter back in the envelope and rising)* I'll make myself some coffee and give Babs a ring. Perhaps we can go at some later time. *(Picking up the envelopes off the coffee-table)* Do you want these? *(He shakes his head. She moves with all the envelopes UC before turning and looking towards the fireplace)* Isn't the rug dry yet?

GYLES: I forgot to check.

ANGELA: *(Opening the door)* Really, Gyles, you're quite impossible! If that stain hasn't come out... *(he looks at her)* I shall feel like spilling your blood not red wine! *(Exits UC, closing the door behind her)*

Left alone, GYLES folds up the newspaper, puts it onto the coffee-table to R of him and sits thinking hard as he stares fixedly towards the fireplace.

After a few seconds, preceded by his shadow, MICHAEL ENTERS R through the french-windows, wearing a pair of jeans with an open-necked, short-sleeved shirt.

MICHAEL: *(Moving in to URC)* A penny for them!

GYLES: *(Rising and moving across to DLC)* That's about all they're worth. You must be exhausted *(MICHAEL reacts)* - after all that chopping. Fix yourself a drink.

MICHAEL: *(Moving to the sideboard UR)* Thanks, I do feel dehydrated, but not through chopping - I couldn't find the axe. Have you seen it? *(Pouring himself a drink)* Want one?

GYLES: *(Momentarily tense; without turning to him)* No.

MICHAEL: The axe or the drink?

GYLES: *(Turning)* Both. I did say not to bother but it should be in the woodshed.

MICHAEL: That's where I looked... obviously not well enough. I'll give it another shot - when I've downed this. *(Carrying the glass he moves to sit in the easy-chair DR)* So I went for a stroll through the woods towards that small lake.

GYLES: We used to go skinny-dipping there - as kids.

MICHAEL: *(Drinking)* We?

GYLES: Er... oh, myself and some of our fair village maidens.

MICHAEL: *(Laughing)* I might have guessed! Only the blondes? But I didn't get that far. The place is swarming with police. They've got the whole area sealed off.

GYLES: *(Suddenly alarmed)* Police! *(Recovering)* What's happened? Has a U.F.O. landed?

MICHAEL: Now that would be something! Apparently a body has been found.

GYLES: *(Half-turning away)* A body!?

MICHAEL: Yes, some chap came across it just before dawn this morning. A poacher I'd imagine, but enough of a responsible citizen to notify the police; although I should think he'd have some difficulty explaining what he was doing in the woods at that hour.

GYLES: Hardly birdwatching! *(Moving apparently casually L of settee to above it)* Where did he find it - in the undergrowth around the lake?

MICHAEL: No, in the shallow water at the edge. It's more like a pond after all this dry weather.

GYLES: I thought you said you didn't get that far?

MICHAEL: *(Taking a drink before putting his glass down onto the coffee-table)* I didn't. I was told by some old dear out walking her dog... an ill-tempered little

Pekinese who stubbornly refuses to respond to the name of Petulia. She took an instant dislike to me. The old dear said it was nothing personal... she hates all men... the dog, not the old dear. Amidst all the nonstop yapping, I gathered that her owner had pumped a young uniformed constable into telling her what he knew about him having been discovered.

GYLES: Him? It was the body of a man?

MICHAEL: Not a doubt about that! Stark naked apparently. The old dear dwelt on that aspect particularly. Probably some repressed 'spinster of this parish' who lavishes all her affection on the unappreciative Petulia, goes to church on Sundays and reads the 'News of the World' afterwards!

GYLES: *(Continuing his move above the settee to look with feigned interest out of the french windows R)* Perhaps he fell in and drowned? Too much to drink at 'The Crown' last night? *(Quickly)* That is, of course, if it happened last night.

MICHAEL: *(Shrugging)* Who knows. At least you'd have an alibi. *(GYLES reacts; MICHAEL rises and moves to DLC)* He was murdered. According to the old dear.

GYLES: How awful!

MICHAEL: I don't know. Depends on one's viewpoint.

GYLES: That's a bit ghoulish, isn't it? *(moving towards DC)*

MICHAEL: *(Turning to him with sudden animation)* It's given me the glimmering of an idea. Amazing how some little incident will trigger things off.

GYLES: I'd hardly call murder a little incident.

MICHAEL: You wouldn't, of course. To me murder is part of everyday life - on the printed page. *(Sitting L end of the settee)* I was thinking of calling it 'Lady in the Lake'.

GYLES: *(Puzzled)* I thought you said it was a man.

MICHAEL: *(Continuing his train of thought)* Too bad Raymond Chandler used that title. 'Woman in the Pond' doesn't have the same ring, does it?

GYLES: *(Sitting in easy-chair DR)* Hardly!

MICHAEL: *(Rising, excitedly)* No, it has to be a woman! Sex and murder... what I need is a titillating title splashed strategically across the ample body of a female nude on the cover... and I could be back in business! Waiting for the royalties to roll in!

GYLES: I never realised what a mercenary chap you are.

MICHAEL: One man's murder is another man's publication cash advance!

GYLES: But you do still have to write it.

MICHAEL: *(Less cheerfully)* Aye, there's the rub! But I can't have lost the knack. *(More brightly)* I haven't felt this good in a long time. At this rate I'll be back at my word processor and Clare and I will be out of your hair... and Angela's, of course. *(Crossing R and above the easy-chair DR to pick up his glass)* In the meantime, I'll have another look for that axe. *(Moving to take the glass up to sideboard UR before turning back to him)* By the way, if it did happen last night, I don't suppose you saw anything suspicious?

GYLES: *(Tensely)* What do you mean?

MICHAEL: When you were out with your lady-friend, whoever she was.

GYLES: No, not a thing.

MICHAEL: Your mind was on other things!?

GYLES: You could say that. Anyway I didn't drive in that direction.

MICHAEL: Perhaps as well. Might have been embarrassing if questioned by the police. Better not mention this to Clare when she gets back - you know how easily she gets upset. *(Looking at his watch)* Shouldn't think they'll be too long now, unless Kate's flight has been delayed.

GYLES: I certainly shan't mention it.

MICHAEL: Kate, I imagine, is made of far sterner stuff, wouldn't you say? I only met her at our wedding, as you know.

GYLES: Yes, of course, that's right. I'd quite forgotten.

MICHAEL: Probably as well not to mention it at all. Murder will out, they say... but why spoil Kate's homecoming - unless you feel like telling Angela?

The door opens and ANGELA ENTERS UC in time to hear the last few words.

ANGELA: Tell Angela what?

MICHAEL: That I'm about to chop her those logs - if I can find the axe.

ANGELA: Is it missing? *(Looking towards Gyles)*

GYLES: So it would seem.

MICHAEL: Probably because I didn't look properly. At least, that's my excuse!

ANGELA: *(Closing the door)* When you find it, do be careful. I shouldn't want Clare ending up without a husband all in one piece.

MICHAEL: I'll try to bear that in mind. Well, this won't keep the home fires burning. See you both later... if I survive! *(Exits through the french-windows)*

ANGELA: *(Moving above settee then down to the fireplace)* He seems very cheerful. *(Examining her hair in the mirror)*

MICHAEL re-enters R, only to briefly look down towards Gyles.

MICHAEL: How's this for a title... 'The Axeman Cometh'? *(Exits R)*

ANGELA: *(Half-turning)* What was that about?

GYLES: *(Picking up the newspaper off the coffee-table)* Michael thinks he's finally come up with the idea for a new book.

ANGELA: About an axe-murderer?

GYLES: *(Off-handedly)* Sounds like it, doesn't it? *(Appearing to start reading)*

ANGELA: Where did that idea come from?

GYLES: How should I know? Where do writers get their ideas? Beats me.

ANGELA: *(Thoughtfully as she turns back to the mirror)* I suppose this means that they will be leaving soon.

GYLES: Shall you miss him?

ANGELA: I was thinking more of you and Clare. *(Turning to him)* But you'll still have Kate.

GYLES: *(Looking up from the newspaper)* What is that supposed to mean?

ANGELA: *(Moving in to below settee)* As if you didn't know! The two of you are thick as thieves. There have been times when I've felt positively de trop. *(Sarcastically)* Will the three of us live happily ever after!?

GYLES: *(Uncomfortably)* Don't talk nonsense!

ANGELA: *(Warmly)* That's my nature, isn't it? Whilst darlin' Kate, the original 'waltzing Matilda' from back of the outback or wherever... she's the prototype no-nonsense, tell-it-as-it-is Australian sheila... isn't she?

Sound of CAR ARRIVING (Offstage R)

That sounds like them now. *(Pause)* Well, aren't you going to greet her with open arms? *(He does not move)* Then I suppose I'd better! *(Moving to exit R through french-windows)*

GYLES: *(Rising quickly and rolling up the newspaper as he strides tensely to the fireplace)* What the hell am I going to do!

CAR STOPS and FEMALE VOICES are heard offstage R. GYLES savagely hits the newspaper against the mantelpiece before throwing it down onto the floor above the easy-chair DL. Reaching a decision, he starts to move quickly L of settee as if making for the door. He checks hastily as ANGELA ENTERS R, followed by KATE HALLORAN and CLARE, the latter wearing a light-weight car coat over a blouse and skirt and carrying a suitcase.

KATE is in her late 30's, a good looking, rather than strikingly beautiful, woman with an aggressively good-humoured manner. She is wearing a linen suit with a neck scarf and is carrying both a shoulder-bag and a flight-bag. Her manner of speech is Australian if not overly so; although at times she appears to deliberately emphasize it for purposes of effect.

ANGELA: *(Moving in to below sideboard UR)* Here she is, Gyles, dear Kate!

GYLES uneasily retraces his steps in front of the fireplace.

KATE: *(Dropping her flightbag by the easy-chair DR)* Large as life and twice as ugly! *(Moving to below settee; as GYLES does not move)* Well, don't I even rate a kiss? *(He moves to L of her and perfunctorily brushes a cheek with his mouth)* Is that all? Hardly worth flying ten thousand miles, give or take the odd thou. *(Turning to Angela and Clare who is standing by the French windows R, having quickly put down the suitcase)* And there I was believing that absence really does make the heart grow fonder! Guess I should have married that handsome sheep farmer after all.

GYLES: *(Making conversation)* How was your flight?

KATE: Bonzer... and that pilot's voice! He could unfasten my seatbelt in any time-zone.

CLARE: *(Protesting)* Kate!

KATE: *(Laughing)* Don't mind my, my darlin'. Flyin' stimulates your old Aunt Kate's libido, or some god-damned thing. Come tomorrow I'll be back to being a respectable old maid.

CLARE: You're not old!

KATE: But, unfortunately, I am respectable!

ANGELA: I'll see about lunch. Are you both hungry?

CLARE: Famished. I was far too excited to eat much breakfast.

KATE: Bless you, darlin'! *(To Angela)* I only hope it's not kangaroo tail soup. I've had enough of that Aussie tucker to last me quite a while.

ANGELA: *(Moving to the door)* I think I can promise you that. *(Exits UC)*

KATE: And what have you been getting up to, Gyles, while I've not been here to keep my beady eye on you?

GYLES: Oh, nothing very much.

KATE: Sounds fascinating! *(Turning to Clare)* Where's that clever husband of yours? Slavin' over a hot typewriter?

GYLES: *(As Clare unhappily fails to reply)* Michael's chopping some logs.... if he's managed to find the axe.

KATE: It's a poor workman...!

CLARE: *(Picking up the suitcase)* I'm going to freshen up, Aunt Kate. Are you coming? *(Moving towards the door)*

KATE: In half a mo. Can you manage that?

GYLES: *(Taking a step forward)* Let me take it, Clare.

KATE: Not tryin' to run out on me, are you, Gyles?

CLARE: It's quite all right - though it is rather heavy.

KATE: *(Smiling)* It's that baby koala I've brought you back. Dump it at the bottom of the stairs. I'll take it up. *(CLARE exits UC with the suitcase. KATE moves UC to close door; fiercely with an immediate change of attitude)* You said she wouldn't still be here!

GYLES: *(Puzzled)* Clare?

KATE: *(Moving quickly DC)* No, not Clare - Darlin' Angela!

GYLES: Where else would she be?

KATE: I don't know and sure as hell don't care! You promised me, Gyles! By the time you get back, you said, she'll have gone - for good. *(He is too mystified to speak)* "Ask no questions", you said, "and then you won't have to tell any lies"!

DOORBELL RINGS (Offstage)

(Picking up her flightbag) Well, there's one question I'm going to ask and when you answer it - I want no lies! Why the hell is she still here? *(Moving UC she snatches open the door and EXITS, leaving the door open)*

GYLES stands, completely perplexed, as ANGELA enters UC

ANGELA: Where's the fire? She almost knocked me over.

GYLES: *(Improvising)* She was in a hurry to have a wash before lunch. Didn't want to keep you waiting.

ANGELA: We shall all have to wait. A policeman is here.

GYLES: *(His eyes momentarily registering alarm before he turns to her, striving to control his tone of voice)* Police?

ANGELA: That's what I said, wasn't it?

GYLES: You'd better ask him to come in.

ANGELA: *(Speaking into the hallway)* Won't you come in?

ANGELA steps aside L to allow DETECTIVE SERGEANT BAKER to ENTER UC. BAKER is in his mid-30's, a pleasant, intelligent-looking man. He is wearing a dark-coloured suit and holding a trilby-hat in one hand.

BAKER: Thank you, ma'am. *(Moving DC and producing his identity-card to hold in Gyles' direction)* Detective Sergeant Baker, sir. Mr. Gyles Fairbairn, I believe?

GYLES: That's right.

BAKER: *(Looking towards Angela)* And this is?

ANGELA: *(As Gyles hesitates briefly)* I'm his wife.

BAKER: Pleased to meet you, ma'am. *(To Gyles)* You don't remember me, do you, sir?

GYLES: *(Warily)* Er, no, I'm afraid not. Sorry.

BAKER: *(Easily)* No need to be, sir. It was a long time ago... all of fifteen years or so, I'd say. I hadn't been long in the Force - just a rookie uniformed constable supposed to merge into the background and only speak if spoken to. Inspector Morton used to say "Keep your eyes and ears open, laddie. Observation - that's the basis of good police work". You'll remember Inspector Morton, of course?

GYLES: *(Uncertainly)* The name does sound familiar.

BAKER: I was with him when he came about... *(hesitating before continuing when Gyles does not respond)* your wife's disappearance. *(Glancing quickly towards Angela)* Your other wife, that is.

GYLES: First wife. I've only had the two... *(attempting a joke)* so far!

ANGELA: *(Looking displeased)* Do you wish me to stay, Sergeant?

BAKER: I'd be obliged if you would.

GYLES: *(Overstating)* We were about to have lunch.

BAKER: In that case I could come back later.

ANGELA: *(Glancing towards Gyles)* Surely there's no need, is there, Gyles? *(To Baker)* We were eating a little earlier than usual. My stepdaughter's aunt has just arrived back from Australia.

BAKER: If that's all right with you, sir? *(GYLES nods curtly) (To Angela)* Perhaps you'd like to sit down. *(Breaking L to below settee)* I'll try not to take too long. *(ANGELA closes the door and moves to sit in easy-chair DRC) (Apologetically to Gyles)* I didn't intend to stir up painful memories for you, sir.

GYLES: You didn't. Won't you sit down?

BAKER: Thank you. *(Waiting until GYLES sits in easy chair DL and then sitting R end of settee and putting hat on the coffee-table R of him)* She never did turn up, did she? Inspector Morton felt sure she would... sooner or later... in one way or another. He never changed his mind on that score, up to the day he retired.

GYLES: How is he?

BAKER: Busy as a bee, sir. Growing roses... taken up bowls. Says he doesn't know how he ever found time to work. *(Producing a notebook in which he proceeds to write from time to time)* But to get to the real reason for my visit...

MICHAEL enters R through the french-windows.

MICHAEL: *(As he enters)* It's no good, Gyles, I can't find that damned axe any...

(tailing off) Sorry, I didn't know you had a visitor.

GYLES: This is Detective Sergeant Baker. *(To Baker)* My son-in-law, Michael Waring.

BAKER: *(Rising)* The Michael Waring? The crime novelist?

MICHAEL: *(Moving to R of him)* Guilty as charged!

BAKER: *(Enthusiastically, shaking his hand)* This is an honour, Mr Waring. I've read every one of your books... with increasing jealousy.

MICHAEL: Really?

BAKER: Your Inspector Dunne never fails, does he? Although I suppose he has one advantage over us mere mortals - his creator always knows in advance who the murderer is.

MICHAEL: *(Smiling wryly)* I wouldn't say quite always. Are you here about the body in the lake?

BAKER: *(With official alertness)* How did you know about that, sir? I doubt whether it's yet made the regional television news.

MICHAEL: I happened to take a walk in that direction earlier this morning.

BAKER: *(With interest)* Did you, sir? Sit down, won't you? *(Moving L to allow MICHAEL to sit R end of settee before himself sitting L end and making a note)* About what time was that?

MICHAEL: *(Thinking)* Let me see... Clare - that's my wife - left about half seven, to pick up her aunt from the airport. *(Baker nods)* I got up half an hour or so later and we had breakfast together. Didn't we, Gyles? *(GYLES nods agreement)* I'd say I ambled off about nine - nine fifteen. Is it important?

BAKER: Not really, sir. I like to get the facts straight that's all. So how did you know about the body? The area was sealed off.

MICHAEL: Some old dear told me... out walking her dog.

BAKER: *(With feeling)* Oh, yes the dog! *(Consulting his notebook)* That would be Miss Jenkinson... Charlotte Emily Anne Jenkinson. She told me her mother was a fervent admirer of the Bronte sisters. You mentioned your wife, sir. Perhaps I'd better have a word with her whilst I'm here.

MICHAEL: Is that necessary? She knows nothing of this morning's events.

BAKER: It's yesterday evening I'm more interested in. She was here?

ANGELA: We went to the theatre.

BAKER: I'd still like a word, if I may?

ANGELA: I'll fetch her. *(Rising and moving to the door)*

BAKER: *(Also rising)* Thank you, Mrs Fairbairn. *(ANGELA exits UC closing the door behind her. BAKER breaking R)* Presumably you all went to the theatre - all four of you?

GYLES: I didn't go.

BAKER: *(Making a note)* Not a theatre-lover, sir?

GYLES: I had a bad cold. Didn't feel up to it. *(MICHAEL quickly suppresses a half-smile)*

BAKER: You appear to have shaken it off well enough. *(Breaking to the French windows R)* Tell me, sir, as a matter of interest, did that brother of yours ever get in touch with you?

GYLES: *(As MICHAEL shows surprise)* My brother?

BAKER: Yes, an identical twin, isn't he? I remember you mentioning him to Inspector Morton. You said he'd swanned off abroad to parts unknown. He had an unusual name...

GYLES: *(Shortly)* Lance.

BAKER: Yes, that was it. He ever turn up?

GYLES: No. Could be dead by now for all I know.

BAKER: I've always understood that twins are automatically aware if something like that happens to the other one.

GYLES: Obviously I must lack that sensitivity.

MICHAEL: *(Unable to contain his interest)* Presuming he is dead. I never knew you had a twin brother, Gyles.

GYLES: *(Uncommunicatively)* Didn't you?

MICHAEL: And Clare has never spoken of having an Uncle Lance.

The door opens and ANGELA enters UC followed by CLARE and then KATE.

ANGELA: *(To Baker as she moves in to above settee)* This is my stepdaughter,

Sergeant, Mrs Waring.

CLARE: *(Nervously as she moves in to below sideboard UR)* I don't know anything.

BAKER: *(Courteously)* Possibly not, ma'am.

KATE: *(Coming forward L of Clare; aggressively)* No possibly about it... there's no cat in hell's chance she knows anything about a murder!

BAKER: *(Quietly)* And you are?

KATE: Her aunt - Kate Halloran.

BAKER: As far as I'm aware, I've made no mention of any murder, Mrs...

KATE: Miss!

BAKER: Miss Halloran. Only that a body has been found.

KATE: Wasn't it murder?

BAKER: As a matter of fact it was. But I'm not suggesting that Mrs Waring is involved. However, it's frequently the case that a person may have some information without being aware of it. Now if I may continue? Please sit down.

KATE solicitously brings CLARE downstage to sit in the easy-chair DR, then herself sits on the upstage arm. ANGELA, after closing the door, moves down L of settee to sit L of Michael.

(Moving in to URC between settee and easy-chair) Our number one priority in a case like this, is to discover the identity of the corpse.

MICHAEL: A male corpse? *(BAKER glances quickly down at him. Explaining)* Courtesy of Miss Jenkinson.

BAKER: That's correct, sir. Can I assume that no male member of this family is missing? *(General silent assent although MICHAEL appears to be about to speak)* Yes, Mr Waring, you were going to say...?

MICHAEL: No, nobody is missing. I was going to ask how the murder was committed?

BAKER: Ah, the murder weapon! *(Lightly)* Always your Inspector Dunne's first thought, isn't it? As a matter of fact, that does lead to a question I have to ask. *(Looking down at Michael)* The man - whoever he may be - was shot... twice... once through the heart. *(CLARE gasps)* At close range.

MICHAEL: There was a struggle?

BAKER: Very likely. A preliminary examination points to the weapon being a .38 handgun of some description. Is there such a weapon in this house? One that may have been stolen? Mr Fairbairn?

ANGELA: *(To Baker, as GYLES hesitates)* I've often told my husband he really ought to have a gun... we're so isolated out here.

BAKER: At least half a mile to the nearest house, I'd say. *(To Gyles)* But you didn't...?

KATE: *(To Baker)* Do you know any man who always does as his wife tells him?

BAKER: *(With a wry smile)* Possibly not - myself included. Well, our men are dragging the lake... what's left of it after all this dry weather... hopefully they may come up with the gun and anything that may help us to identify the body. Clothes, for instance... he wasn't wearing a stitch.

KATE: No nudy colony around these parts, is there, Gyles? I might think of joining.

MICHAEL: *(To Baker)* Can't the body tell you anything?

BAKER: You know what they say, sir... 'dead men tell no tales'. The M.E. says it appears to be of a man in his mid-40's...

KATE: A dangerous age, eh, Gyles?

BAKER: Healthy-looking, without any distinguishing features. No moles, tattoos, operation scars...

MICHAEL: *(To Baker)* Not very co-operative is he! Presumably, of course, his dental records will enable you to obtain confirmation of his identity.. once you get a lead as to who he may be?

BAKER: There's a major snag there, sir... The corpse is minus a head!

CLARE: *(Amongst general reaction)* Oh, no!

MICHAEL: Someone really is making things difficult for you.

BAKER: Even Inspector Dunne wouldn't find it easy-going, would he? When you first came in, sir, I believe you mentioned not being able to find an axe.

MICHAEL: That's right. Angela *(glancing towards her by his side)* ... Mrs Fairbairn... wanted me to chop some logs.

ANGELA: It's nice to have a willing volunteer. *(Looking towards Gyles)* My husband made such a fuss over the last lot.

BAKER: When was that, sir?

GYLES: *(Edgily)* I really don't remember... does it matter?

BAKER: *(Patiently)* I was only trying to establish when the axe was last seen.

ANGELA: It was only a few days ago. My husband quickly tired.

BAKER: *(To Gyles)* Where was it kept?

GYLES: *(Tersely)* In the woodshed. Where the devil else?

BAKER: Is it kept locked?

MICHAEL: It isn't actually a shed... just a lean-to roof against one of the outbuildings.

BAKER: So anyone could have come along and helped themselves to the axe?

CLARE: *(Puzzled)* But why would anyone...?

BAKER: The Medical Examiner says that an axe could have been used...

CLARE: *(Jumping up)* How horrible!

KATE: *(Standing to comfort her)* Do you have to be so callous!?

BAKER: *(Uncomfortably)* I'm sorry, but Mrs Waring did ask...

ANGELA: *(Impatiently)* For heaven's sake, don't be such a baby, Clare! It's not as if it's anyone you know.

CLARE: *(Protesting)* It might be!

KATE: *(Rudely)* Get off your bike, Angie! You can see she's upset.

ANGELA: She's easily upset. *(Angrily)* And don't call me Angie!

KATE: *(Smiling)* Just one big happy family, eh, Serge? *(With an arm round Clare as if to take her to the door)* You won't be needing her any more, will ya?

BAKER: *(Politely but firmly)* I'm afraid I shall, if you don't mind.

MICHAEL: *(As Kate is about to speak)* Sit down, Clare, the Sergeant's only trying to do his job.

BAKER: *(As Clare reluctantly sits)* Thank you, sir. But I shan't be needing you, Miss Halloran. I understand you only arrived back in the country this morning?

KATE: If Clare stays - I stay! So you're happy with my alibi?

BAKER: *(Drily)* Unless you're clever enough to be in two places at the same time. The approximate time of death has been estimated at between eight and ten o'clock yesterday evening, at which time you were...?

KATE: *(Flippantly)* Winging my way back here up in the bright blue yonder.

BAKER: *(Gravely)* Murder does happen to be a very serious business, Miss Halloran.

KATE: *(Unchastened)* It is for the victim.

BAKER: And the accused!

ANGELA: *(Pointedly)* You must excuse Kate's offbeat sense of humour, Sergeant. It remains obstinately Australian after all the years she's lived here.

BAKER: *(Attempting to pacify the situation)* That's quite all right, ma'am. Nothing like having a sense of humour - whatever the nationality. *(Looking at his notebook)* So, recapping... yesterday evening Mrs Fairbairn and Mr and Mrs Waring visited the theatre, Mr Fairbairn did not and Miss Halloran was up in the bright blue yonder...

KATE: Sampling the duty free.

BAKER: At what time did the theatre-party leave?

ANGELA: About seven, wasn't it, Michael?

CLARE: Nearer ten past... waiting for you. I was quite sure we were going to be late.

ANGELA: That's nothing new! You always find something to worry about.

BAKER: *(Stepping in tactfully)* And what time did you get back?

ANGELA: Now that I can be quite sure about. The hall-clock started to strike midnight as we came in.

BAKER: And Mr Fairbairn was here waiting for you?

ANGELA: No, he wasn't.

BAKER: *(Alert)* Really? *(Looking with interest towards Gyles)*

GYLES: I was having a bath. I thought a good long soak would help me shake off the worst effects of that cold.

BAKER: And it certainly worked, sir, didn't it? I presume that, as you didn't feel well enough to go to the theatre, you were here the entire evening?

GYLES: *(After the briefest hesitation during which he and Michael exchange a barely perceptible glance)* Of course.

BAKER: *(Moving L above the settee)* Did you hear anything at all suspicious... any shots?

GYLES: No, but I was playing some music most of the time. *(Indicating the music-centre on the small table UL)*

BAKER: Anything in particular?

GYLES: *(With a nervy little laugh)* Do you know, I'm blowed if I can tell you. *(Half-picking up the book off the coffee-table)* I was reading this latest book of Michael's.

BAKER: 'Model for Murder' *(To Michael)* Don't know how he does it - your Inspector Dunne. I never guessed the identity of the murderer.

MICHAEL: *(Jokingly)* When in doubt, go for the character least likely.

BAKER: If only it was that easy in real life! *(To Gyles)* So there's nothing at all you can tell me?

GYLES: Afraid not, sergeant. Sorry I can't be more helpful.

BAKER: That's all right, sir. Don't worry about it. *(Moving back above settee to UC)* As for the others - excluding Miss Halloran of course - did any of you notice anything at all unusual, either before leaving for the theatre, or when you got back?

CLARE reacts intensely, unseen by him.

ANGELA: Only my missing rug.

BAKER: What was that, ma'am?

GYLES: *(Quickly)* I may as well own up. I had a little accident - spilt a glass of red wine on it. It's in the cellar drying.

BAKER: *(Not showing interest)* And that's all? *(Closing notebook)* I don't suppose there had been any strangers about at any time yesterday? *(Aware of Clare's further reaction)* Yes, Mrs Waring?

CLARE: *(Nervously)* Well... it was probably nothing.

BAKER: *(Prompting her)* Let me be the judge of that.

CLARE: *(Rising and looking away from him)* Probably just my imagination.

MICHAEL: Of which my wife is well endowed, Sergeant.

ANGELA: *(To Clare)* If you've got something to say - for heaven's sake, say it!

KATE: *(Sharply)* Why don't you leave her alone! *(Gently to Clare)* Was it something you saw, darlin'?

CLARE: *(Nodding her head)* It was as we were driving away for the theatre... I thought I saw something in the bushes at the bottom of the drive.

BAKER: Something... what was it?

CLARE: I'm not sure. *(After a barely perceptible sideways glance in the direction of Gyles)* It looked like a figure of a man.

BAKER: Did you see his face?

CLARE: No, not really. It looked as if he was trying to hide.

ANGELA: Why on earth didn't you say something?

CLARE: *(Defensively)* You'd only have said I was imagining things, as usual.

BAKER: *(To Michael)* Did you see anything, sir?

MICHAEL: No. I was driving.

BAKER: Well, if there really was somebody there, that might explain the missing axe.

MICHAEL: Which would seem to indicate that the murder was premeditated... assuming of course there is a connection... not merely a coincidence?

BAKER: Don't hold much store in them myself - although I have known your Inspector Dunne be grateful for one.

MICHAEL: Touché! A lucky coincidence does occasionally come in useful to a crime novelist when his plot gets stuck.

BAKER: In which case I must remember to come to you, sir, when I get stuck! *(Putting notebook away)* I think that's all. If you do find the axe, I'd be pleased to know... would eliminate that line of enquiry. *(After brief pause)* By the way, it would seem that the perpetrator we're looking for is left-handed... judging from the entry and exit bullet wounds, that is.

KATE: That let's you off the hook, Gyles - as the angler said to the mermaid!

ANGELA: *(To Baker)* My husband is right-handed, Sergeant.

BAKER: *(Lightly)* I'm pleased to hear it. Not, of course, that he was under any suspicion... *(as an unthinking comment as he takes his hat from the coffee-table C)* on this occasion.

GYLES: *(Startled)* What is that supposed to mean?

BAKER: *(Embarrassed)* Sorry, sir, that slipped out. Please forget it.

GYLES: *(Angry)* I'm damned if I will! I demand to know what you meant.

BAKER: *(Miserably)* I had no right to say it.

MICHAEL: *(Forcefully)* But you did say it!

BAKER: Not in the first place. It was Inspector Morton. It became quite an obsession with him.

KATE: C'mon, Serge, you can't chicken out now.

BAKER: *(Reluctantly to Gyles)* It was in connection with your first wife's disappearance, sir.

CLARE: My mother's disappearance? What about it?

BAKER: *(Unhappily)* I don't want to upset you, ma'am.

KATE: The harm's already done. *(To Clare)* Come and sit down, my darlin'. *(Gently pulling her down into the easy-chair)*

MICHAEL: *(Evenly)* I really do think you ought to tell us. Not knowing will only make things worse.

BAKER: *(Still hesitant)* I suppose you're right. You see, Inspector Morton was quite convinced in his own mind that... *(moving above settee to R in order to address Gyles rather than Clare)* well, that your wife was dead, sir, and that you... *(tailing off)* .

GYLES: That I'd killed her?

CLARE: *(Horrified; amidst general reaction)* Daddy, you didn't!

BAKER: *(Shamefaced)* Look, I really am terribly sorry but you did insist. And now that Inspector Morton is retired - it was something I heard him say - on more than one occasion. Personally, I don't know whether there was any shred of evidence but he kept the file open in case she ever... *(tailing off again)* .

MICHAEL: Of course there was no evidence! Just forget about it, Gyles.

BAKER: *(Apologetically)* I'd best be going before I put my foot in it again. *(Taking out notebook and writing before tearing out the page)* This is the telephone number of the Incident Room we've set up in the village. If anyone should think of anything else, I'd be obliged if you'd give us a ring. *(Holding out the page towards Gyles)*

ANGELA: *(Taking it when Gyles does not)* I'll see you out. *(Rising)*

BAKER: *(Moving above settee to C as he puts notebook away)* No, that's all right, ma'am. If you don't mind I'll slip out this way *(indicating the french-windows)* and take a look in those bushes at the bottom of the drive. Never know what I might find.

MICHAEL: *(Jocularly as he rises)* A thread of cloth snagged on the holly bush... a stamped out cigarette... with or without a lipstick's traces!?

BAKER: *(Smiling)* I should be so lucky! My name's Baker don't forget - not Dunne. And only Sergeant at that.

KATE: This could be your lucky break. Get your cuffs on the murderer and it might be Inspector Baker. How's that sound, Serge?

GYLES: At some other poor devil's expense?

BAKER: *(Equably)* There is that way of looking at it, sir.

MICHAEL: Still, that's the name of the game, isn't it?

CLARE: *(Intensely)* You call it a game!?

BAKER: No, ma'am, it's no game. Anyway, Chief Inspector Woolley is in charge of the investigation. I'm just one of his dogsbodies. I'd like to thank everyone for their co-operation and I really am sorry to have delayed your lunch. I hope you enjoy it. *(Starting to move towards the french-windows R)*

ANGELA: *(Moving above the settee)* You're quite welcome to join us.

BAKER: Thank you, ma'am, but I feel I've already outstayed my welcome. I'll wish you all "Good day". *(Exits R through the french-windows)*

He is followed by a chorus of farewells from ANGELA, KATE and MICHAEL, with CLARE and GYLES remaining silent.

ANGELA: I'll put this number by the phone just in case. *(Putting the page of* *notebook on the sideboard UR)*

CLARE: *(Emotionally, as she springs to her feet and crosses downstage towards Gyles in the easy chair DL)* What a beastly, horrible thing to say! *(Dropping down onto her knees at his feet)* As if you could kill anyone... let alone Mummy! Why didn't you tell him it wasn't true! It can't be true! *(Starting to weep as she clings to his knees)*

KATE: *(Rising off the arm of the easy chair DL)* Of course it isn't true, Clare.

MICHAEL: *(To Clare)* The Sergeant didn't say it was. He was only telling us what the Inspector said.

ANGELA: *(Stepping forward to UC)* Must we have all this fuss about something that happened years ago?

GYLES: *(After momentarily looking as if he was going to sympathetically stroke Clare's bowed head, he rises abruptly)* I thought we were going to have lunch?

KATE, ANGELA and MICHAEL watch in silence as GYLES quickly moves L of settee to open the door and exit UC.

KATE: Nothing like a spot of excitement to stimulate the appetite.

CLARE: *(As Michael tries to help her to her feet)* I'm all right. *(Struggling slowly to her feet and moving L of settee to above it as he then follows her to L of settee; checking)* There was something I didn't tell that Sergeant.

KATE: What was it, my darlin'?

CLARE: The man I saw in the bushes...

MICHAEL: *(Prompting her)* What about him?

CLARE: *(Tightly)* He looked just like Daddy! *(as ANGELA looks at her with a painfully eloquent expression; shrilly)* Go on, why don't you say it!?

ANGELA: You know perfectly well that Gyles was here, in this room, when we left. I do wish you'd pull yourself together! *(CLARE, without another word, turns on her heels and runs out of the door to Exit UC. ANGELA to Michael)* Now she's started seeing things! *(Exits UC)*

KATE: She's always been highly-strung, but this is going a bit far. *(Moving up to the door where she looks back towards MICHAEL standing deep in thought)* You comin' to put your bib and tucker on?

MICHAEL: *(Vaguely)* I'll be right there. *(KATE exits UC. MICHAEL looks around musing and unfocussed until his eyes lower to gaze fixedly down to his feet where the hearthrug should be and then, after a second or two, he lifts his head, deep in thought)* I wonder....? Surely not...! *(As he starts to turn slowly to look towards door UC)*

CURTAIN

ACT II Scene 1

After lunch. AT RISE: *The stage is empty. The door is closed. The french-windows remain open but SUNLIGHT no longer enters.*

After a few seconds the door opens and MICHAEL ENTERS UC, closing it behind him. During the brief time that it is open FEMALE VOICES are heard (offstage). MICHAEL strolls to look out of the french-windows R, registering the fact that he is feeling uncomfortably hot. He crosses below the settee to DL where, retrieving the newspaper from the floor by the floor-lamp, he sits in the easy-chair and begins to turn the pages in a rather desultory manner. After a few seconds the door opens again and ANGELA ENTERS UC. The FEMALE VOICES are again heard (offstage) and, with a sigh of relief, ANGELA closes the door to shut them out.

ANGELA: *(Leaning against the door)* I'd almost forgotten how Kate can chatter... yabber as she calls it. At times she seems to be speaking a foreign language.

MICHAEL: *(Idly scanning the pages)* Yes, she does rather go on a bit, doesn't she?

ANGELA: *(Crossing to the french-windows R)* Go on a bit! And Clare hangs onto her every word - the gospel according to Saint Kate!

MICHAEL: *(Folding up the newspaper)* Hardly strikes me as a likely candidate for canonization... far too worldly-wise and attracted to the sins of the flesh, I should imagine. Odd she's never married. *(Placing the newspaper on the coffee-table to L of him)*

ANGELA: According to her it's certainly not for want of offers. She's regaling Clare now about this sheepfarmer she met from Western Australia... *(imitating Kate)* 'a right old battler he was, just wouldn't take "No" for an answer - no matter what the question! I told him there wasn't a snowball's chance in hell I was ever goin' to find myself stuck on some jimbuck station at the back of beyond and if he thought otherwise, he'd got roos in his paddock!'

MICHAEL: *(Smiling)* Sounds as if Clare could do with an interpreter.

ANGELA: *(Looking out of the open windows)* It's become stifling hot all of a sudden, hasn't it?

MICHAEL: Shouldn't be surprised if we're not in for a storm.

ANGELA: *(Moving to sit in the easy-chair DR)* Where's Gyles?

MICHAEL: Haven't a clue. Not seen a sign of him.

ANGELA: He couldn't wait to get into the dining-room, but then he hardly ate a thing.

MICHAEL: *(Rising)* No, he was behaving rather strangely. That Sergeant's visit seemed to upset him. *(Moving L of settee to above it)* Understandable, I suppose. Couldn't have been exactly pleasant discovering that one might have been the Number One suspect in your wife's murder - if she had been. Apart that is from having been reminded of what must have been a harrowing experience.

ANGELA: *(Thoughtfully)* It never seemed to be worrying him unduly when we first met. He hardly ever mentioned her.

MICHAEL: What about his brother?

ANGELA: *(Surprised)* His brother? *(Firmly)* He hasn't got a brother!

MICHAEL: *(To UC)* Oh, yes he has... at least he did have. An identical twin.

ANGELA: You must be mistaken.

MICHAEL: No, I'm not. He is called Lance. Sergeant Baker asked Gyles about him. Seems he'd been mentioned at the time Clare's mother disappeared.

ANGELA: You mean he was involved?

MICHAEL: No, he'd left the scene before that happened. Gyles thinks he must be dead - not having heard from him all this time. And Gyles has never mentioned him?

ANGELA: Not a word.

MICHAEL: *(Moving down to L of her)* Doesn't that strike you as being odd? I mean twins are supposed to be so close, aren't they? From the womb onwards.

ANGELA: *(Rising and moving below him to DLC)* Gyles has always been something of a law unto himself. Why don't you ask him if you're interested?

MICHAEL: Why don't you?

ANGELA: I'm not particularly interested. And you're the one addicted to solving mysteries.

MICHAEL: *(Smiling)* Having first created them.

ANGELA: Which reminds me - Gyles says you've got the idea for a new book. Does this mean you'll be leaving?

MICHAEL: *(Lightly)* Trying to get rid of me?

ANGELA: *(With feeling)* You know that's not true! *(Breaking L)* I can't bear to think what it will be like here without you - the three of us, Gyles, Kate and me.

MICHAEL: *(Moving to R of her)* You knew it would have to end sometime.

ANGELA: *(Fiercely)* Why should it? If only Gyles would disappear! And take Kate with him. *(Sitting L end of settee)*

MICHAEL: That would still leave Clare.

ANGELA: You don't love her!

MICHAEL: *(Matter of fact)* She is my wife.

ANGELA: *(Mockingly)* Till death us do part?

MICHAEL: That wasn't very funny. *(Sitting R of her)* I think you're wrong about Gyles and Kate... there being anything between them.

ANGELA: Why?

The door UC starts to open quietly and then is held slightly ajar by an unseen person.

MICHAEL: I hardly think Kate's absence has made Gyles' heart grow fonder - if it ever was. He's lost his heart elsewhere - much closer to home than Australia.

The door closes with a barely audible CLICK.

ANGELA: *(Rising quickly)* What was that? *(Looking upstage)*

MICHAEL: What was what?

ANGELA: I thought I heard the door close.

MICHAEL: *(Rising and moving UC)* It is closed. *(Opening it and looking out)* Nobody there. *(Closing the door)* You're getting to be as jumpy as Clare.

ANGELA: Heaven forbid! I don't want to start imagining things - mysterious figures lurking in the bushes.

MICHAEL: *(Moving DC)* If she was imagining it.

ANGELA: *(Incredulously)* Looking just like Gyles?

MICHAEL: I must admit that did seem to be overdoing it.

ANGELA: I don't know how you put up with her moods.

MICHAEL: At times neither do I.

ANGELA: What did you mean about Gyles having lost his heart closer to home?

MICHAEL: *(Moving L below her; with feigned indifference)* Oh, that? Forget it... just a little joke between the two of us. *(Sitting in easy-chair DL)* I tease him about not being able to keep his eyes off one of the barmaids down at the pub.

ANGELA: *(Moving to DC)* The one with the cleavage like the Cheddar Gorge?

MICHAEL: *(Laughing)* Babs.

ANGELA: *(Turning to him)* So you've noticed it too?

MICHAEL: I should have to be deaf and dumb as well as blind... ! I'm sure there's nothing for you to be worried about.

ANGELA: *(Vigorously)* Who said I was worried! *(Turning quickly to move UC)* If those two have finished yakking I'll see about clearing away. *(Opening the door)* They might even condescend to help! *(Exits UC, closing the door behind her with a bang)*

MICHAEL gives a wry smile, moves below settee to DC, looks around thoughtfully and then moves purposefully to the sideboard UR. He is examining the bottles as GYLES ENTERS R through the french-windows.

GYLES: *(Entering)* Help yourself.

MICHAEL: *(Startled)* What!? Oh, no, thanks. *(Breaking L above the settee)* Bit too early for me.

GYLES: *(Moving in to the sideboard)* I think I will. Turned damned close out there... *(pouring a drink)* really oppressive.

MICHAEL: *(Moving down L of settee)* Been for a walk, have you?

GYLES: Yes, didn't feel much like eating. Thought a breath of fresh air might do me good. Not that there was any.

MICHAEL: *(Sitting in easy-chair DL)* Probably in for a storm.

GYLES: *(Moving DRC with glass in hand)* That's why I came back. It's black as night over in the direction of the village and I thought I felt a spot or two of rain.

MICHAEL: *(Smiling)* Unless it was the gnats jimmy-riddling?

GYLES: *(Sitting in easy-chair DR)* Could be... plenty of the little devils about. *(raising glass to drink)*

MICHAEL: Up by the lake?

GYLES: *(Checking with glass in mid-air)* What?

MICHAEL: I thought perhaps you'd gone in that direction? They're usually attracted by water.

GYLES: As a matter of fact, I did go up that way. *(Drinks)*

MICHAEL: *(Lightly)* Returning to the scene of the crime? *(As GYLES quickly stares at him)* It was a joke. Sorry!

GYLES: I'm the one who should apologise... seem to be a little on edge.

MICHAEL: *(Easily)* Probably the weather. It does affect some people that way.

GYLES: *(Vaguely)* Yes. *(Sipping his drink abstractedly)*

There is a pause.

MICHAEL: } There's something I'd like to...
GYLES: } By the way I meant to... after you.

MICHAEL: *(With a hand gesture)* No, please...

GYLES: I was only going to say I wanted to thank you.

MICHAEL: For what?

GYLES: Not saying anything when I told the Sergeant I'd been here all evening.

MICHAEL: We men must stick together. Perhaps we ought to form a trade union? The way the feminist movement is progressing we shall all end up as second-class citizens in one way or another... housepersons... baby-sitters. Let's hope it never gets as far as childbearing!

GYLES: *(Rising to take glass back to sideboard UR)* Still it's never a good idea, is it... lying to the police?

MICHAEL: Not generally speaking, no.

GYLES: *(Hesitantly)* Obviously, it would have been terribly embarrassing... telling the truth. And possibly implicating the lady in question.

MICHAEL: It wasn't as if you were in need of an alibi, was it?

GYLES: *(With a vaguely uneasy laugh)* Of course not. Anyway, thanks. I didn't mean to inadvertently end up getting you involved.

MICHAEL: *(Laughing)* As an accomplice after the fact? I sincerely hope not. Light adultery is one thing... murder an altogether different kettle of fish.

GYLES: *(Changing the subject and starting to move towards DC)* What were you going to say...?

MICHAEL: It was something I was going to ask... about your brother.

GYLES: *(Suddenly checking)* My brother!

MICHAEL: Yes, the one Sergeant Baker asked about. *(As Gyles hesitates)* Of course, if you'd rather not...? It's just that I find myself intrigued - call it a writer's insatiable curiosity - why you never talk about him. I can't speak for Kate, but it seems both Clare and Angela didn't even know he existed.

GYLES: *(Moving above settee)* In one way that's the point... does Lance exist? I doubt it very much.

MICHAEL: *(Rising and moving thoughtfully to DRC)* But you don't know for certain? *(Turning to him)* Were you two completely identical?

GYLES: *(Moving to L of settee)* Oh, yes, in every way. Physically at least... like the proverbial peas in a pod. Even our voices sounded alike. At school we used to drive the teachers frantic. Or rather Lance did. He was always up to some mischief - for which I invariably got the blame. He thought it was great fun.

MICHAEL: What happened to him?

GYLES: There was a hell of a row... just before our twenty-first birthday. I'd already gone into the family business. Father wanted Lance to do the same - to get married and settle down. Lance had other ideas, wanted to see the world he said... told Father he'd rather be dead than spend his life sitting behind a desk. Father told him if that was his attitude he'd better get out... that he never wanted to see him again. *(Sitting on L arm of settee)* Things might have been different if Mother had still been alive - Lance had always been her favourite.

MICHAEL: So he left?

GYLES: *(Grimly)* Oh, yes, he left! After telling Father what he thought of him. Father was furious - I don't think he'd ever been spoken to like that before. After that he would never allow Lance's name to be mentioned again. I suppose it became second nature for me not to do so. *(Rising)* Not that we were ever very close; nevertheless, I'm not particularly proud of the fact. Only goes to show what a weak character I am.

MICHAEL: That I should never have guessed!

GYLES: Anyway, it's too late for me to reform now. *(Sitting in easy-chair DL)*

MICHAEL: Let sleeping dogs lie?

GYLES: As well as dead brothers?

MICHAEL: You really are sure? That he is dead, I mean?

GYLES: Oh yes. There are times when I have this strange feeling of loss - it's something I've never admitted to anyone before - and of not having a sense of my true identity. You probably won't believe this, but when I looked in the shaving-mirror this morning, I found myself wondering... who am I? Am I really Gyles... or could I be Lance?

MICHAEL: *(Smiling)* And you told Sergeant Baker you lacked sensitivity! What conclusion did you reach?

GYLES: When the razor nicked my face I knew I was me!

MICHAEL: I'm glad - not that you cut yourself! And speaking of cutting - there's still those logs need doing if I can find the axe.

GYLES: I shouldn't bother. It's far too hot for us to want a fire this evening.

MICHAEL: Still, I'll have another scout around. *(Moving to the french-windows R)* Would be rather gruesome, wouldn't it, if it did turn out to be the one the police are looking for? *(Exits R)*

GYLES rises and, crossing downstage, he pulls out and sits on the bureau chair DR. Finding some notepaper and a pen he proceeds to write left-handed with deliberation. The door opens and KATE ENTERS UC. Concentrating hard, GYLES is unaware as she closes the door without a sound and moves down to behind the easy-chair DR.

KATE: *(Looking down)* What's all this... practising signing your autograph for when you hit the headlines?

GYLES: *(Startled)* For having done what?

KATE: How the hell should I know what you've been up to whilst I've been away. And why with your left hand?

GYLES: I... er, seem to have sprained my right wrist. Don't know how. Can't hold the pen properly and Angela's been on to me about writing a cheque to pay the electricity bill.

KATE: *(Forthrightly)* Well, one thing's for sure, I wouldn't recommend signing the cheque like that.

GYLES: Why not?

KATE: Why not!? I could make a better forgery with both eyes closed.

GYLES: It's hardly a forgery. It's my signature.

KATE: Looks nothing like it. *(Moving above the easy-chair to C)* If you don't want anybody asking awkward questions I'd wait until your right wrist's not crook. I'm surprised you don't pay by direct debit.

GYLES: *(Putting pen down)* That's not a bad idea. *(Checking to see that Kate is not watching, he folds up the notepaper and slips it into his pocket)*

KATE: *(Sitting L end of settee)* I'm full of them, didn't you know? How did you come to do it - sprain the wrist? *(As he stands and pushes in the chair)* Did she put up a fight? Or did you get too rough?

GYLES: Who?

KATE: *(Sarcastically)* Whoever the lucky lady is.

GYLES: I don't know what you mean.

KATE: *(Aggressively)* Come off it, Gyles! Sure you do.

GYLES: *(Moving in to DRC)* Look, if you've got something to say - for heaven's sake spill it out!

KATE: *(Rising)* Alright, cobber, I will. Who's the sheila you've been screwing while I've been away? Or perhaps there's been more than one?

GYLES: Who have you been talking to... Michael?

KATE: So he knows all about it, does he?

GYLES: *(Breaking R)* He seems to think he does. The whole thing's ridiculous.

KATE: So now I'm ridiculous, am I? That wasn't what you thought of me before I went away. You certainly have changed your tune, Gyles. You're like a different person.

GYLES: Now you really are being ridiculous.

KATE: *(Strongly)* Am I? *(Moving to DC)* Well, 'scuse I, but did we or did we not have an understanding? *(As he does not reply)* We most certainly did! And you're going to stick to it... or else the band will play! *(More calmly as she breaks towards DL)* OK, we'll say no more about what you may or may not have been up to. And I haven't been strictly celibate myself for the past three months. But now I'm back and here I stay. You owe me something, Gyles Fairbairn - you owe me one helluva lot! And I mean to have it. All those years I slaved looking after Clare. Oh, I was glad enough to do it and a good job too - Angela had about as much motherly instinct as a dried-up billabong. Couldn't wait to marry her though could you, as soon as Jenny was declared legally dead. But how long did it last before you tired of her? And then turned to me. Very convenient, wasn't I? It so happened you were what I wanted - had wanted for some years. And that is what I intend to have... you, Gyles, all to my little ownio!

GYLES: Have you quite finished?

KATE: *(Forcefully)* No, I'm not finished, not by a long chalk! *(Moving to confront him DRC)* You promised me that Angie wouldn't still be here when I got back. Well, I am - and so is she! Don't tell me you've changed your mind about doing whatever you intended? Was there going to be another mysterious disappearance - just like Jenny?

GYLES: *(Moving below her towards DL)* What do you mean?

KATE: *(Turning to him)* If I thought for one minute there was any truth in what that policeman said... ! *(With controlled vehemence)* I'm warning you, Gyles, if I ever found out you'd done anything to harm one hair of Jenny's head - I'd have your guts for garters! You'd find yourself suddenly parting company with a certain part of your anatomy... or should I say parts? *(With an obscene but* *eloquent hand gesture)* How would that grab you!? Choir practice would never be quite the same! She was my sister... Clare's mother... Don't you ever forget that - not ever!

The door opens and CLARE ENTERS UC.

CLARE: *(Sensing the tension)* Is there something wrong?

KATE: *(Quickly relaxing)* No, my darlin', why should there be anything wrong? Me and your father was just having a good old yabber about things... what he's been up to - *(pointedly)* or not up to. That's fair dinkum, eh, Gyles?

CLARE: *(Moving in to above settee)* We've been keeping an eye on him for you, Aunt Kate.

KATE: *(Breaking DR)* Goodonya!

ANGELA ENTERS UC through open doorway.

CLARE: *(To Angela)* Haven't we?

ANGELA: Haven't we what?

CLARE: Been seeing that Daddy hasn't been getting into any mischief?

GYLES: I can see I'm getting outnumbered. Time to beat a hasty retreat. 'He who fights and runs away...' *(Moving C and then towards french-windows R)* I'll take a turn round the garden. Then you can talk about me to your heart's content. *(Exits R)*

KATE: As if we've nothing better to do! Men really think they're the bees' knees, don't they? Or the cat's whiskers! Still I guess they're a necessary evil.

CLARE: *(Seriously)* I don't know what I should do without Michael.

KATE: How about you, Angela? Could you do without Gyles?

ANGELA: *(Moving above settee and below Clare to UL)* Oh, I think I might manage.

KATE: That's the spirit! Men... who needs 'em? *(Moving UC)* Come on, young Clare, you can help me unpack. I might just find a present I smuggled through the Customs for you.

CLARE: *(Excited)* What is it?

KATE: *(As Clare exits UC)* Wait and see! *(Exits UC, leaving door open)*

There is a FAINT RUMBLE OF THUNDER. ANGELA moves to the french-windows R and stands looking out and upwards. After a few seconds, MICHAEL ENTERS UC through the open doorway. He is looking seriously thoughtful as he carries a small rug.

ANGELA: *(Turning as she hears him close the door)* I thought I heard a rumble of thunder. Did you?

MICHAEL: I was in the cellar.

ANGELA: *(Moving in to URC)* My rug! It's ruined, isn't it?

MICHAEL: What makes you say that?

ANGELA: The look on your face.

MICHAEL: *(Moving above settee to L of it)* As a matter of fact it isn't. See for yourself. *(Opening and displaying the rug before spreading it out in front of fireplace)*

ANGELA: *(After moving to below settee; delighted)* That's marvellous! You wouldn't know any wine had been spilt on it.

MICHAEL: *(Soberly)* If it was wine!

ANGELA: Of course it was. You heard Gyles say that he'd spilt some red wine.

MICHAEL: *(Pointedly)* Which normally he doesn't touch. Do you see any? *(Indicating the sideboard UR)*

ANGELA: *(Moving to sideboard and examining bottles)* No, there isn't - only some white... that Palette we like from Provence. He must have finished off a bottle of red.

MICHAEL: In which case, where's the empty?

ANGELA: Does it matter? In the garage I suppose, waiting to go to the bottle-bank in the village.

MICHAEL: *(Moving to below settee)* It isn't. There aren't any. Gyles and I took some the morning before last.

ANGELA: *(Moving DC; disinterestedly)* So he's absentmindedly put it somewhere else. Who cares?

MICHAEL: Do you remember what you said last night? That if this was in one of my books the reason for the disappearance would have been because it was bloodstained.

ANGELA: You mean Gyles broke the glass and cut himself? There's no sign of it. And if he had, why not say so - why just say that he'd spilt some wine?

MICHAEL: *(Crossing below her towards DR)* Perhaps that was all that he did. A forensic test might or might not now prove otherwise.

ANGELA: *(Protesting)* Mickey, this isn't one of your books! *(Breaking L below settee)*

MICHAEL: *(Perching on arm of easy-chair DR)* He lied to the police, you know. About not having gone out last evening.

ANGELA: But he didn't!

MICHAEL: He did. His car was moved after we left for the theatre. That was why I took so long when we got back. He hadn't left me much room to get in.

ANGELA: *(Breaking to fireplace L)* I don't understand... he said he wasn't well enough to go with us...

MICHAEL: That's what he said!

ANGELA: Are you saying he invented having the cold. Why?

MICHAEL: *(Hesitating, as he stands)* Where is he now?

ANGELA: In the garden.

MICHAEL: *(After moving to look out of french-windows R)* Can't see him. *(Hesitantly as he moves in C)* Look, I did promise Gyles I wouldn't say anything, so this is between the two of us. OK? *(Pausing as ANGELA nods)* I jokingly accused him of having an affair... of deliberately getting out of going to the theatre so he could indulge in a spot of light - or heavy - dalliance.

ANGELA: *(Looking down at the rug on which she is standing)* Here!?

MICHAEL: No, not here. *(Slightly embarrassed)* I wasn't suggesting that sort of evidence. He drove somewhere... presumably not too far away because of the time element.

ANGELA: What did he say?

MICHAEL: He didn't deny it - not finally. Oh, he huffed and puffed a bit at first, but eventually he admitted it.

ANGELA: Did he indeed! But why lie to the police?

MICHAEL: That is obvious. He didn't want anyone else to know... you, Clare... Kate.

ANGELA: But surely wasn't lying about it dangerous? After all it is a murder enquiry.

MICHAEL: Certainly not advisable... unless one happens to be involved.

ANGELA: Which Gyles isn't. If you knew, why did you keep quiet?

MICHAEL: I'm not my father-in-law's keeper. Why rock the boat over a harmless flirtation? Which doesn't seem to bother you.

ANGELA: Why should it? But you don't seem to happy about it.

MICHAEL: *(Thoughtfully)* No, I'm not... not entirely. I don't know why... if only I could put my finger on it. There's something vaguely troubling me.

ANGELA: If you think he might have been lying to you as well as to the police, why don't you ask him... ask him what really happened last night?

There is a louder RUMBLE OF THUNDER as GYLES ENTERS R through the french-windows.

GYLES: *(As he enters)* Sounds as if that storm's coming this way. At least we can shut it out. *(Closing the french-windows)*

ANGELA: *(Pointedly, as she moves above settee towards the door)* Do you think so? *(Opening door)* You always were an optimist, weren't you? *(Glancing back at MICHAEL as he moves L to fireplace. She EXITS UC closing door behind her)*

GYLES: *(Puzzled)* Was that supposed to be meaningful in some way?

MICHAEL: *(Lightly)* Don't ask me. I gave up trying to understand women when I was about sixteen.

GYLES: *(Moving DRC)* Very wise. The harder you try the less you... *(tailing off as he notices the rug on which Michael stands)*

MICHAEL: *(Stepping upstage off the rug as he sees where Gyles is staring)* Cleaned up quite well, didn't it? You made a good job of that, Gyles.

GYLES: *(Adopting a light attitude)* Didn't I just! *(Breaking DR)* Do you think I missed my true vocation?

MICHAEL: *(Moving below settee)* It looked quite dry so I thought I'd bring it up.

GYLES: *(Sitting in easy chair DR)* Thanks.

MICHAEL: Don't mention it. I happened to be in the cellar... thought the axe might somehow have found its way down there. It hasn't.

GYLES: I must remember to get another.

MICHAEL: Looks as if someone has walked off with it. Perhaps Clare's mystery figure hiding in the bushes?

GYLES: If she really did see someone.

MICHAEL: Oh, I think she did. Clare's highly imaginative, but not to the extent as to tell the police. Don't suppose you saw anybody lurking about when you took the car out?

GYLES: Not a soul... all was quiet.

MICHAEL: As a grave! *(Strolling casually round L of settee to above it; with a smile)* You know there was something Clare didn't tell the Sergeant... didn't want to look ridiculous. In fact, she lied - she did see the man's face. She said he looked like you.

GYLES: *(With a nervous laugh)* Me!? No wonder she didn't want to feel ridiculous. I'm not an illusionist. Haven't yet mastered the art of being in two places at the same time. Could be a useful trick.

MICHAEL: Angela accused her of seeing things that didn't exist. Even Kate agreed.

GYLES: *(Rising)* That makes it unanimous, doesn't it? *(Crossing downstage to DL. He checks his move to avoid stepping onto the rug)*

MICHAEL: *(Carrying on his move to UC)* Not quite unanimous, Gyles, I feel convinced she did see someone.

GYLES: *(Turning to him)* Looking like me? *(Protesting)* Come on, Michael! How did I do it - with mirrors? You saw me - here in this room.

MICHAEL: Yes, you were here... but I have a theory - far-fetched as it may sound.

GYLES: *(Restrained)* Let's hear it... however far-fetched.

MICHAEL: *(Moving slowly by degrees to below settee)* Clare has never known that she had an uncle... an uncle who was your identical twin. Do you see what's in my mind?

GYLES: *(Curtly)* Lance is dead.

MICHAEL: *(Persisting)* What if he isn't? For argument's sake let's say he's still alive. Wouldn't that explain... logically explain... why Clare thought the figure in the bushes looked like you? *(Gyles remains silent)* It was Lance, wasn't it? Lance was here last night, wasn't he, Gyles?

GYLES: *(Hesitates and then moves below Michael to DRC; reluctantly)* Alright, he was here. *(Tensely)* Are you satisfied?

MICHAEL: *(Firmly)* No, I want to know what happened.

GYLES: *(After a pause)* Do you! Apparently, he was in some god-forsaken spot in South America trying to scrape a living - more of an existence by the sound of it - when quite by chance he came across an old English newspaper someone must have had sent out there. There was the announcement of Father's death and the fact that he'd left everything to me.

There is another RUMBLE OF THUNDER, even louder this time, as MICHAEL sits on the settee.

(Continuing) Lance took it pretty badly. *(Moving to french-windows R; musingly as he looks out)* Don't suppose I can blame him really - *(half turning)* me getting all the money, the house, the family business... the lot! *(Turning back to look out)* I probably would have felt the same way. Still he'd made his bed... *(moving in to URC)* Anyway he dropped everything - not that he had much to drop - and managed to work his way back here. He arrived late yesterday afternoon and hid in the bushes to keep watch on the house, trying to discover exactly who was here. He must have thought it was his lucky day when he saw the three of you drive away. *(Starting a move to take him by degrees above the settee and then L of it)* Angela must have left a chink in the curtains when she closed them and, damned fool me, I hadn't locked the french-windows. He saw I was alone and the first thing I knew there he was. *(gesturing R)* I thought I was seeing a ghost but he quickly made me realise he was very much alive. He quizzed me as to who you all were in the car. I told him - and about Jenny's disappearance. He asked me where you'd gone and when you'd be back. *(Moving to below settee DC)* Then he told me why he'd come... he wasn't interested in this house or the business... all he wanted was what he called his half of Father's money. I told him he'd forfeited that claim years ago. Still, he was my brother and, judging by his clothes and overall appearance, in pretty

much of a bad way. I offered to give him a thousand pounds of my own money on condition that was the last I'd see of him. He turned nasty and made it quite clear what I could do with the thousand pounds... he demanded his half share of Father's money... not a penny less. I refused... Father had been adamant. I told him he should have thought of that before he went storming off in a rage all those years ago. Then he produced a revolver... he said I'd better think again and be damned quick about it. *(Breaking DR)* I was sitting there *(indicating easy-chair DL)* I'd been reading your book...

MICHAEL: And drinking red wine?

GYLES: There was no red wine. It was the first excuse that came into my head. He came towering over me... pointing the gun at me... and talking wildly. *(Demonstrating, as if using gun with left hand)* I was convinced he was going to shoot me. I made a grab for the gun as I leapt to my feet. There was a struggle. His finger was on the trigger but somehow I'd turned the barrel towards his chest. Suddenly the gun fired - twice! His grip on it relaxed, leaving the revolver in my hand. Then he slumped to the floor - there on the rug! *(Gesturing L before sinking into the easy-chair DR)* He was dead!

MICHAEL: *(Rising)* Why didn't you call the police?

GYLES: *(Miserably)* I should have done, of course. I realise that now. In one way I panicked... thinking what effect it would have on Clare - the inquest, perhaps even a trial if the police didn't believe my story. The shock would have been too much for her.

MICHAEL: *(With feeling)* I see your point. *(Breaking DL)* Not that I think you did the right thing. After all, it was self-defence. So what did you do?

GYLES: Opened the windows, picked up the gun - I'd dropped it after the shots - carried him to the garage and got him into the boot of the car.

MICHAEL: And drove off?

GYLES: *(Hesitating)* After first collecting the axe from the woodshed.

MICHAEL: *(Aghast)* You don't mean...? The body in the lake?! *(GYLES nods almost imperceptibly)* He was your brother, for Christ's sake!

GYLES: *(Rising quickly)* Yes, my identical twin brother! What else should I have done? I might as well have left my visiting card.

MICHAEL: *(Incredulously)* How could you?

GYLES: Needs must when the devil drives. And I certainly felt I was being driven by the devil. None of it was my fault, Michael. I hadn't asked him to come back. Damn it, for years I'd felt sure he was already dead. *(Moving UC)* I stripped off his clothes, brought them back and burned them in the boiler-fire.

MICHAEL: What about the gun, the axe... his....?

GYLES: Let's just say that I disposed of them all. It might not be wise for me to say anymore.

MICHAEL: Don't you trust me?

GYLES: I don't know.

MICHAEL: You certainly had a busy evening.

GYLES: You can say that again! *(Moving back DC)* When I came back I noticed there was some blood on the rug. I cleaned it off and took it down to the cellar to dry. I was just coming back up when I heard your car. I raced upstairs, stripped off and took a quick shower.

MICHAEL: What happens now?

GYLES: *(Resignedly)* That's up to you.

MICHAEL: *(Surprised)* Why me!?

GYLES: Are you going to inform the police?

MICHAEL: Gyles, you're my father-in-law! *(Moving UL of settee)* I wish to God you hadn't told me!

GYLES: You were the one who wanted to know.

MICHAEL: *(Uneasily)* And now I do know and, if I continue to keep quiet, that would make me an accessory after the fact... an accessory to what is being regarded as murder.

GYLES: *(Protesting)* But it wasn't! I've told you what happened - you have my word.

MICHAEL: But would the police accept your word? You lied to them about not going out last evening... and you lied to me, which was why I kept quiet in the first place. A romp in the hay - or the back seat of your car - was one thing. But the suspicion of murder... ! Don't you see, what you ended up doing would be interpreted as an admission of guilt... guilty of having shot Lance in cold blood and then... *(suddenly stopping)*

GYLES: Now what?

MICHAEL: *(After a pause)* Why the left hand, Gyles?

GYLES: I don't understand.

MICHAEL: Just now, when you were demonstrating what happened... struggling with Lance... you used your left hand to hold the imaginary gun.

GYLES: *(Equivocating)* Of course. Lance was left-handed - the only way in which we differed physically speaking. I was showing you how he held the gun, pointed at me, in his left hand.

MICHAEL: *(Thinking hard)* And the police are looking for a left-handed killer.

GYLES: So?

MICHAEL: So, I can't pretend to be an expert, but I don't see how that ties in with what you told me.

GYLES: *(Bluntly)* In other words, you don't believe me!

MICHAEL: I didn't say that, did I? Let me show you what I mean... Say I'm Lance *(demonstrating)* with the gun in my left hand pointing at you. Now you made a grab for it... how? Do it! *(GYLES does so, using both hands on the imaginary gun)* I see - with both hands. But, as your right arm will dominate the muzzle will turn towards his chest like this. *(Demonstrating)* So when the gun fired, surely it would appear to have been done by a person holding it in his right hand?

GYLES: *(Beginning to bluster as he breaks away DR)* I've told you what happened... Lance was holding the gun in his left hand.

MICHAEL: *(Continuing to think the matter out)* I believe you. But, assuming the police are correct about the trajectory of the bullets and it being a left-handed person, then Lance must have been pointing the gun away from him towards... ! *(moving to sideboard UR)*

GYLES: *(With sudden urgency)* What are you doing?

MICHAEL: I'm phoning the police.

GYLES: *(Forcefully)* No, wait! I'm Clare's father!

MICHAEL: *(Coldly as he picks up telephone)* Are you? Are you really? Where's that phone number?

GYLES: *(As MICHAEL takes the page of notebook off the sideboard; with total resignation)* Alright, you win! I'm Lance Fairbairn. Gyles is dead. He deserved to die!

There is a FLASH OF LIGHTNING, followed immediately by a LOUD CRACK OF THUNDER as if overhead.

MICHAEL turns slowly towards him and then 'freezes' with the telephone in his hand.

CURTAIN

ACT II Scene 2

IMMEDIATELY AFTERWARDS. AT RISE: *MICHAEL and LANCE (GYLES) hold their positions - at sideboard and DR respectively. CLARE screams (Offstage) and both men turn as the door flings open and CLARE ENTERS UC, checking on the threshold, wide-eyed with fear. There is another FLASH OF LIGHTNING followed by a LOUD CRACK OF THUNDER. Galvanised into action CLARE runs forward and throws her arms around the startled LANCE, burying her face into his chest.*

LANCE: What's the matter? What's wrong? *(Slowly relaxing a little he gradually lifts his arms from their stiff position at his sides and tentatively cradles her body with growing tenderness)*

MICHAEL: *(Quickly putting telephone down, steps forward)* It's the lightning. *(Firmly drawing her out of Lance's grasp)*

CLARE: I can't stand it. You know I can't! *(Breaking away from both of them towards DL)*

ANGELA ENTERS UC

ANGELA: Who's being murdered? *(Seeing Clare)* Oh, it's you, Clare! *(Moving to UR of settee)* I might have known.

As LANCE stands dismayed , KATE ENTERS UC and moves immediately

61

above and L of settee to take Clare into her arms.

KATE: *(Comfortingly, as if to a child)* There, there, my little darlin', it'll soon be over.

CLARE: *(Sobbing)* They don't care... nobody cares!

KATE: *(Soothingly)* Of course they do. Michael cares... and your father cares. Don't you, Gyles?

LANCE: *(Awkwardly)* Of course.

KATE: *(Derisively)* Angela pretends not to understand.

ANGELA: *(Unsympathetically)* There's no pretence about it.

KATE: There was a thunder storm the day Jenny disappeared - a real boomer, I'm led to believe. Ain't that so, Gyles?

ANGELA: *(Irritably, as Lance hesitates)* Yes, I've heard that before - many times. Too many times!

MICHAEL: *(Mildly reproving)* Steady on!

ANGELA: *(Hotly)* What do you mean "steady on"? She gets on my nerves.

There is another FLASH OF LIGHTNING followed after a short interval by THUNDER now less loud.

KATE: *(As Clare clings to her)* What did I tell you? It's moving away. What say we go in the kitchen and close the curtains and have a nice cuppa of camomile tea. (Starting to lead her gently L of settee then above it towards the door) That always helps calm you down, doesn't it? Anybody care to join us? (There is no response) Suit yourselves!*

KATE and CLARE EXIT UC through the open doorway.

MICHAEL: *(To Angela)* Don't you think you should apologise?

ANGELA: *(Firmly)* No, I don't! *(As he continues to stare fixedly at her)* I've a feeling you want to get rid of me. What are you two up to?

MICHAEL: *(With mock light touch as he looks towards Lance)* Discussing a case of murder.

ANGELA: *(Not taking him seriously)* Who has Gyles supposed to have killed? Or shouldn't I ask? At least a wife can't give evidence against her husband, can she? *(Exits UC)*

MICHAEL: *(After moving to close the door)* You really are Lance? That wasn't a sick joke?

LANCE: *(Crossing downstage to below settee; grimly)* A joke! More of a nightmare! I'm Lance... I assure you.

MICHAEL: *(Moving DC)* It's amazing! You look and sound so alike.

LANCE: A pity we didn't think alike.

MICHAEL: And you killed him? Your own brother... Clare's father!

LANCE: *(Opening mouth then pausing before speaking with obvious change of mind. Dully)* You'd better call the police. Let's get it over with.

There is a faint RUMBLE OF THUNDER as LANCE sinks onto L end of settee. MICHAEL starts to move upstage towards the sideboard then checks.

MICHAEL: It can wait. *(Inquisitively, as moves DC)* I want to know what really happened - the truth this time.

LANCE: It started out as I said. My life was at an all time low ebb when I read about Father's death. Always going to strike it rich tomorrow, next week, next month, next year... sometime never! *(MICHAEL unobtrusively sits in easy-chair DR)* And I wasn't getting any younger. I realised there would be far fewer tomorrows, less and less next years. I was feeling desperate and then... out of the blue! Not a mention that I existed - ever had existed. Dear Gyles had got the lot. I determined then and there to get my share. *(Rising and moving L of settee and then above it to UC)* I had no money. I almost stowed away but ended working my passage on an old tub held together by rust and barnacles. One whiff of a storm and she'd have gone to Davy Jones' locker. *(Bitterly)* A pity she didn't! I felt sure that Gyles would do the decent thing by me - but I brought along my revolver just in case. The places I'd been you need one to stay alive.

MICHAEL: So you came prepared to kill him?

LANCE: *(Firmly)* No, I didn't! Only to threaten him if necessary. I swear I never intended to use it... he was my brother, my twin brother! And they say that blood is thicker than water! *(To DC)* There was no fraternal offer of the thousand pounds. He just laughed at me... laughed in my face! He told me to get out. I pulled out the gun to scare him. He said I hadn't the guts to use it. He was right... I hadn't! *(Moving below the settee towards easy-chair DL)* I put the revolver down on this table *(miming the action with left hand)* and turned to slink away with my tail between my legs. *(Moving to DC)* It was then he told me.

MICHAEL: *(Absorbed)* Told you what?

LANCE: About him and Jenny. He could see he'd won but that wasn't enough for him. He could be a sadistic devil. He wanted to grind my nose in the dirt. *(Moving UC to above settee)* You see all those years ago, Jenny and I were lovers. We intended to get married. Gyles was madly jealous... not used to playing second fiddle - especially not to me. Father liked the idea of becoming Jenny's father-in-law, but not through her marrying me. Oh no, it had to be Gyles! And that suited him down to the ground. He callously set about destroying our relationship - turning Jenny against me in any way he could. He used his charm on her... and he could be quite ruthlessly charming when he wanted to be - as no doubt you know? *(MICHAEL nods assent)* *(Moving L of settee)* Like the fool I was, I played right into his hands... giving him Jenny on a silver platter. I had this row with Father. He ordered me to stop seeing her. And on top of that, there was the business of me going into the family concern. If I didn't he said I'd to clear out - that he never wanted to see me again. *(Slipping into silence)*

MICHAEL: *(Prompting him)* And Jenny married Gyles?

LANCE: *(Sinking into easy-chair DL)* Not long afterwards, it seems. Everything worked out perfectly for him - or so it seemed at the time.

MICHAEL: What happened?

LANCE: Apparently she was pregnant before they married.

MICHAEL: It does happen!

LANCE: Gyles told me he didn't know... until later. That child wasn't his. Jenny tricked him. She married him to give the child his name. He never forgave her for that. From then on the marriage was doomed and so, after Clare was born, was Jenny.

MICHAEL: *(With growing apprehension)* What do you mean?

LANCE: *(Rising)* Gyles killed her!

MICHAEL: *(Appalled)* He killed her! *(Rising)* She didn't just disappear? But why, even if Clare wasn't his...

LANCE: At some point Jenny told him the truth... that I was Clare's father!

MICHAEL: Was it true?

LANCE: It could have been. But I didn't know. Do you think I'd have gone away if I had? That was something Gyles could never forgive - or forget! Last night, it gave him intense pleasure telling me. I saw red, I don't mind admitting. He'd destroyed Clare's mother because I was her father. I felt like destroying him with my bare hands. *(Moving in to below settee)* I turned towards him and found him pointing my revolver at me. I lost control and leapt at him. There was a brief struggle. I had the advantage as I was on my feet; he was still sitting in the chair. Suddenly, I found the gun in my hand. *(Demonstrating with left hand)* I fired twice. He slumped out of the chair onto the rug. *(Staring down at the rug before turning to him)* The rest was as I told you... except the body was Gyles. He deserved to die for killing Jenny.

MICHAEL: *(Stunned)* How did he...?

LANCE: I don't know. I didn't want to know. But he weighted her body and threw it into the lake. That was what gave me the idea of doing the same.

MICHAEL: *(Grimly)* So I was right... the lady in the lake! *(Moving to look out of the french-windows R; turning after a thoughtful pause)* But why didn't you just vanish into the night?

LANCE: That's what I've been asking myself all day... why?... Why?... WHY? If only I'd stopped to think but there was this voice inside my head saying, "You've come halfway across the world to get what you feel is morally - if not legally - yours. You didn't want this to happen - you didn't intend this to happen - but it has happened. Why not take advantage of it. Don't just walk away!"

MICHAEL: So you decided to masquerade as Gyles?

LANCE: I didn't decide... it wasn't a conscious decision on my part. I merely acted, like being on automatic pilot. What a fool I was!

MICHAEL: *(Moving to DRC)* Surely you'd never have got away with it... for any length of time? Trying to live another person's life.

LANCE: You needn't rub it in! It certainly wasn't to be a long-term thing. Just long enough to get some of the money I felt was mine... perhaps cash a large cheque... *(producing the paper from his pocket)* Kate caught me trying to forge his signature. I pretended to have sprained my right wrist.

MICHAEL: Take the money and run!

LANCE: That's what I should have done... run while I had the chance.

MICHAEL: *(After a brief pause)* What's stopping you now?

LANCE: You're going to call the police. You are going to call, aren't you?

MICHAEL: *(Uncertainly)* I wish to God I knew! You have been telling me the truth?

LANCE: *(With sincerity)* The whole truth and nothing but the truth. Do you believe me?

MICHAEL: Yes, I think I do. And as Clare's father... well, it puts me in something of a quandary, doesn't it?

LANCE: What would you tell her if I was to disappear? Unless you told her the truth she'd think that, as Gyles, I was her father. To have one parent disappear seems to still affect her. Another could be too much. On the other hand, if you did tell her the truth - that the man she's always thought was her father isn't really - but killed her mother?

MICHAEL: And that her real father is actually the uncle she never knew she had, but killed the man she thought was her father - but now is her dead uncle! That ought to be more than enough to have her on a psychiatrist's couch for the rest of her life!

LANCE: *(Explosively)* Why the hell did I come back! I've messed up all your lives... Clare's in one way or another... Kate's - it seems she and Gyles had quite a thing going.... Angela - I've made a widow of. And now, I've got you involved in all my troubles.

MICHAEL: A trouble shared...

LANCE: *(Firmly)* No, I got myself into this. *(With abject resignation)* You better had phone the police.

MICHAEL: And what will you tell them? That it was an accident? You came here with a loaded gun... To them that will spell one thing - premeditation. And as if that wasn't enough, you tried to conceal the crime. In their book that's the action of a guilty man.

LANCE: Which is what I am. *(Sardonically)* But I thought one was presumed innocent until proved otherwise!

MICHAEL: That's in a court of law and I wouldn't give much for your chance of proving yourself innocent if it was true. It would be manslaughter at least. As I see it, there's only one thing for you to do... get away... now... today... before it's too late. If they do discover the identity of the body the game's up.

LANCE: What about Clare? She's my daughter.

MICHAEL: And my wife. If I keep quiet then your disappearing act will be by far the lesser of the two evils. Don't you agree?

As LANCE pauses, trying to reach a decision, the door is opened by KATE who then stands aside to allow CLARE to ENTER UC, carrying a tray with two cups and saucers, small milk-jug, sugar-basin and a teapot. LANCE breaks L towards the fireplace as CLARE moves downstage to place the tray onto the coffee-table R of the settee.

KATE: *(Closing the door)* Will you look at this - waitress service, no less. Aren't you the two lucky jackaroos?

MICHAEL: *(To Clare)* Feeling better?

CLARE: *(Moving to L of him)* Yes, thank you. I'm sorry I made all that fuss. *(Turning to include LANCE who tensely does not respond)*

KATE: *(Moving down to above the coffee-table C)* You'll grow out of it one of these fine days - provided nothing else traumatic happens. Shall I be mother? You can leave your tips under the saucer! *(MICHAEL sits easy-chair DR as KATE proceeds to pour two cups of tea)* My little darlin' thought you must be more than ready for a smoke-o... tea-break to you ignorant Pommies. And I was wondering what on earth you were finding to talk about all this time - talk about women yabbering. *(To Michael)* Milk and sugar?

CLARE: *(Before he can answer)* Just a spot of milk. He's watching his waistline.

MICHAEL: *(As she sits on upstage arm of chair)* Correction - she's watching my waistline!

KATE: *(Pouring milk)* And quite right too. *(To Lance)* Angela ought to be doing the same. I suppose it still is plenty of milk and two sugars, Gyles?

CLARE: *(As he does not respond)* Daddy! Aunt Kate's speaking to you.

LANCE: *(Back to earth)* What? Sorry!

KATE: Thought you'd gone walkabout. Milk and two sugars?

LANCE: *(Without thinking)* No... *(quickly)* I mean, yes.

KATE: Make up your mind, cobber! *(Pouring milk and adding two spoonfuls of sugar)*

MICHAEL: Where's Angela?

KATE: *(Offhandedly)* Don't ask me. Seemed a bit miffed... said she wasn't going to sit drinking tea in the kitchen with the curtains closed like a scared child. *(Handing Michael's cup and saucer to Clare)* That should wet his whistle.

MICHAEL: *(Taking cup and saucer from Clare)* Thanks.

KATE: *(Bringing the other cup and saucer to below the settee)* Looks as if you could do with this, Gyles.

LANCE: *(Stepping forward to collect cup and saucer)* Thanks.

KATE: *(To him as she sits R end of settee)* You can sit down... *(Patting seat of settee)* I shan't bite.

LANCE: *(Hesitantly)* I'll sit here... then I can use the table. *(Sitting easy-chair DL and putting cup and saucer on the coffee-table)*

KATE: Suit yourself. I haven't brought back the plague... not that I know of.

CLARE: *(As Gyles and Michael drink)* Aunt Kate! How I've missed you.

KATE: That's a relief! *(Glancing pointedly towards Lance)* I was beginning to feel about as welcome as a blowfly at a barbie!

There is a brief awkward pause during which the two men drink.

(Whispering conspiratorially to Clare) You know, I think we interrupted something, darlin'. *(To Lance)* Do tell - or is it a secret?

MICHAEL: *(Stepping in as Lance hesitates awkwardly)* Not exactly. I was telling Gyles about the idea I've had for a new book.

CLARE: *(To him)* That's wonderful! What's it about?

MICHAEL: *(Putting cup and saucer onto coffee-table)* Basically, a man in a difficult dilemma. You see, he's killed another man. As a matter of fact, his brother - his identical twin brother.

CLARE: *(As Lance puts cup and saucer onto coffee-table rather noisily)* How horrible!

KATE: *(After glancing towards Lance)* So why's he up a gum tree?

MICHAEL: For reasons of his own he's assumed the identity of the dead man, but now can't make up his mind what to do for the best. At present the police don't know what he's done - but that might well not last. There's nothing to stop him making a break for it - not physically - but psychologically he's worried of the effect that might have on someone he cares about very much.

CLARE: *(As Lance desperately tries to appear normal and relaxed)* And were you asking Daddy what he thinks he should do... this man?

MICHAEL: He was about to tell me when you came in.

KATE: Well, Gyles, don't keep us in suspenders - what do you reckon this bonzo ought to do?

As LANCE rises tautly and impulsively the door opens and ANGELA ENTERS UC.

ANGELA: That policeman's here again... asking to see you, Gyles.

LANCE: *(Trying to appear calm after hurriedly glancing towards Michael)* Ask him to come in. *(Sitting again)*

ANGELA: *(Turning to speak to offstage)* Come in, please, Sergeant. *(Moving to above settee)*

BAKER: *(Offstage)* Wait there, Constable. I'll give you a call should I need you.

MALE VOICE: *(Offstage)* Very good, Sergeant.

BAKER: *(As he enters UC, looking serious and carrying his hat)* Good afternoon, everybody. *(Closing the door)* I'm sorry to have to disturb you all again. *(Moving downstage to between Clare and Kate)*

KATE: Brought reinforcements, have you, Serge?

BAKER: *(Politely formal)* In a manner of speaking.

KATE: I promise to go quietly.

BAKER: I'm pleased to hear it. *(With scarcely hidden feeling)*

CLARE: *(Tentatively)* Did you find anything... in the bushes I mean?

BAKER: I'm afraid not, Mrs Waring. The ground's much too hard to show footprints. There could have been someone there.

CLARE: *(With nervous intensity)* There was! I know there was. I saw him!

BAKER: *(Tactfully)* I wasn't doubting your word, ma'am. Anyway, it's more tha~~n~~ likely he'll be far away by now.

MICHAEL: Always assuming he had any connection with what happened.

BAKER: That's true, sir. Otherwise he may well still be in the vicinity. But it seen~~s~~ highly likely to me that was how and why Mr Fairbairn's axe disappeared. ~~In~~ which case the connection is obvious.

KATE: *(Facetiously)* Unless he had this rampant urge to chop down a tree!

BAKER: Then why bury the axe?

ANGELA: How do you know he did?

BAKER: Because one of our men found it - and the gun - scarcely hidden un~~der~~ some rotting leaves near to the lake. Looks to have been done in rather a hu~~rry~~

MICHAEL: Have you found anything else?

BAKER: *(Glancing quickly at the ladies)* I see what you mean. No, sir, not as ~~yet.~~ *(Turning to Lance)* You may be asked to make an identification, Mr Fairba~~irn.~~

LANCE: *(Startled)* Of the body?

BAKER: Hardly. I meant to identify the axe - if it's yours. Not that it's releva~~nt~~ just to give us some idea as to the killer's movements.

MICHAEL: And the gun - was it...?

BAKER: The murder weapon? Not much doubt of that, sir. A .38 revolver with ~~two~~ rounds fired. We shall know for certain after the post-mortem.

LANCE: Then you're certain it was murder? I mean, might it not have bee~~n an~~ accident... in the first place?

BAKER: That would be for a jury to decide.

MICHAEL: If you find the killer.

BAKER: As you say, sir. And until - or if we know the identity of the victim~~ that~~ would appear unlikely.

ANGELA: But surely, Sergeant, someone must know something - if only ~~... that~~ some person who is missing. Don't you think so, Michael?

MICHAEL: *(Studiously avoiding eye-contact with Lance's anxious glance~~)~~*

direction) It's possible.

BAKER: Well, let's hope they do! I hardly imagine the killer will be foolhardy enough to walk in and confess. *(More briskly)* However, that wasn't why I came back, I'm afraid.

CLARE: *(With intuitive apprehension)* It's bad news, isn't it?

BAKER: *(Soberly)* Yes, ma'am, it is. Our men have been dragging the lake - what there is left of it.

KATE: And...?

BAKER: We found a lot of stuff you might expect - old tyres... a broken pram... bicycle wheel.

KATE: An untidy lot, you Poms.

BAKER: *(Trying to be patient)* We also found something we didn't expect... didn't want. Another body, or rather the remains of what was once a body. It must have been there for a good many years. *(LANCE looks at him)* The M.E. says it was a woman... a youngish woman.

ANGELA: I don't understand, Sergeant. You said you'd come to see my husband.

BAKER: That is correct, ma'am. *(Hesitating; and then tactfully)* Perhaps it would be as well if you and the other ladies would withdraw.

KATE: *(Forthrightly)* That's a sexist remark, if ever I heard one!

BAKER: This is hardly the time to worry about being politically correct or otherwise.

KATE: Well, I for one am staying put.

BAKER: *(To Angela)* Mrs Fairbairn?

ANGELA: *(Less firmly)* So am I. *(Moving to sit on L arm of settee)*

BAKER: *(Turning to Clare)* How about you, Mrs Waring? *(CLARE gives a tense, nervous nod)* Very well. *(Putting his hat on the coffee-table C before moving above settee; to Lance)* How old was your first wife, sir, at the time she went missing?

KATE: *(Promptly; as Lance hesitates)* My half-sister was twenty-three - almost twenty-four. I remember I'd already bought a birthday card when I heard the news back in Australia.

CLARE: *(Apprehensively to Baker)* What makes you ask that?

BAKER: *(Hesitating awkwardly)* I'm afraid you're going to find this mos distressing.

CLARE: *(Steeling herself and grasping Michael's hand)* I want to know!

BAKER: *(Reluctantly)* The remains we found... they would appear to have been o your mother.

KATE: *(As Clare gasps)* How can you know that?

MICHAEL: Dental records?

BAKER: *(Nodding assent)* I said earlier that Inspector Morton was convinced sh wasn't still alive. He obtained her dental records in case... They were on fil which has now been checked. We're regarding it as a case of murder.

KATE: *(Wildly to Lance as she jumps to her feet)* Then you did kill her, yo bastard! Bloody bastard!! *(Looking as if on the verge of physically attackin him as CLARE bursts into tears)*

BAKER: *(Hurriedly running DC to restrain her)* Madam, please! Contro yourself!

ANGELA stares horrified at Lance as MICHAEL stands and sits CLARE in th easy-chair before moving R to behind it and placing his hands on he shoulders.

KATE: *(Struggling against Baker's restraining hand)* I hope they bring bac hanging. No, that's too good for you. If I had my way...!

BAKER: Miss Halloran! *(Forcing her down onto the settee)* Miss Halloran, if yo don't sit down and keep quiet I shall have to ask the constable to remove yo

CLARE: *(Sobbing to Michael)* Tell him it isn't true... it can't be true!

ANGELA: It isn't true, is it, Gyles?

KATE: *(Vindictively)* Of course it's true! Look at him - it's written all over hin He's guilty as hell!

MICHAEL: You don't know that.

KATE: *(Snarling to Baker)* Well, what are you waiting for, Serge? Aren't yo going to arrest him?

BAKER: Madam, do you mind? *(Officiously)* Gyles Fairbairn, I must ask you accompany me.

LANCE: *(Slowly getting to his feet)* Am I under arrest?

BAKER: No, sir, not at present. You're required for questioning in connection with the disappearance and death of your wife.

KATE: *(Incredulously)* You mean... you're not arresting him?

BAKER: *(Trying to remain patient)* I'm carrying out my orders, ma'am. The rest will be up to Chief Inspector Woolley. *(Firmly to Lance)* Now, sir, I trust you'll come along quietly?

LANCE: *(Protesting)* But I'm not the man you want. I didn't...

MICHAEL: *(Interjecting quickly)* I'd be careful what you say, *(with slight emphasis)* Gyles. *(As Baker looks questioningly at him)* Without your solicitor present. That is right, isn't it, Sergeant?

BAKER: Yes, sir, quite right. *(Turning to Lance)* But it isn't a question of identity, is it? Only a matter of guilt. This way, sir, if you please.

KATE glares hatefully at him as LANCE slowly moves below settee to DC. As he does so BAKER picks up his hat and starts moving towards the door, keeping an eye on him. LANCE pauses to look down at the sobbing CLARE and involuntarily reaches out a hand towards her.

CLARE: *(Hysterically)* Don't touch me! *(Recoiling and sidling out of the chair)* You killed my mother! My own father! How could you? *(Backing towards french-windows R)* Keep away from me! I never want to see you again! *(Wrenching open one half of the windows and running to Exit R)*

MICHAEL: *(Sympathetically, as he moves above easy-chair DR towards him)* I'm sorry that happened.

LANCE: *(With quiet irony)* Understandable, wasn't it? *(Starting to hold out his left hand and then his right)* Thanks! *(MICHAEL shakes the hand firmly)*

BAKER: *(Opening the door)* We're coming out now, constable. You can be starting the car.

MALE VOICE: *(Offstage)* Righto, Sergeant.

LANCE looks silently at Kate and Angela, then moves to the door. BAKER stands aside to allow LANCE to pass him and EXIT UC. With a nod of acknowledgment BAKER turns to leave.

ANGELA: *(Rising from the settee-arm)* Sergeant!

BAKER: *(Checking)* Yes, Mrs Fairbairn?

ANGELA: Will he... will my husband be coming back?

BAKER: This evening? Let's say - I shouldn't wait up. *(EXITS UC, closing th door behind him)*

There is a pause

ANGELA: *(Breaking DL)* Do you really think he did it, Michael?

KATE: *(Viciously)* Of course Gyles did it - who else?

MICHAEL: *(Sardonically; moving slowly DC)* Who else indeed!

Sound of car starting up and driving away.

CURTAIN

Other NPN Plays by Jack Booth
Full Length Plays

254 Sleeping Arrangements 3M 4F

Hollywood star Kathleen Fenton is upset when, visiting England with prospective husband number 3, she discovers as her mother's guest ex-husband number 1. Her annoyance grows as the men hit it off and plan filming together. When Kathleen's glamour photographer father arrives with a model in tow and ex-husband number 2 appears, the general tension increases with sleeping arrangements becoming of paramount concern.

332 Tangled Web 3M 3F

Ex-mercenary soldier Ian Millward has heavy gambling debts. Now a photojournalist, he ostensibly arranges to interview wealthy Sir Robert Darwent but actually intends to blackmail him over revealing photographs taken of his wife Anne years ago when Ian's lover. But Sir Robert also has a past indiscretion to hide and Ian increasingly finds himself enmeshed, leading to a highly dramatic and unforseen dénouement.

One Act Plays

300 By Whose Hand 5F

On an evening in the late 1940's the Fairclough women leave the menfolk to their after-dinner drinks. The drawing-room tranquility is broken by the arrival of a German-speaking woman seeking revenge for her sister's murder during the war. One of three men in the house was the killer. Amidst revelations and rising tensions the question is... by whose hand?

257 Dead On Time 1M 3F

A wealthy but ruthless industrialist is being the victim of threatenin phone calls. He is told that by two o'clock next morning he will be dead man. The police are called in and members of his household ar questioned. The deadline approaches but nothing untoward occurs. I it the work of a crank... or may he still be "dead on time"!?

314 Echo of Applause 3M 2F

On a provincial stage the show is over - closure and demolition wi follow. Tony has vainly struggled to save both theatre and his blighte career. In despair he seeks the solace of alcohol and rejects on woman's advances. Tony himself may be saved by a girl's innocent lov but the theatre will be left with its ghosts and an echo of applause.

316 Friendly Affair 4F

Newly-pregnant and highly-strung Glenda has a problem - suspiciou lipstick on her husband's collar. Panic-stricken, she summons for hel - her more experienced older sister, her man-loving best friend and th dominant wife of Martin's best friend in whom he may have confided h infidelity. Misunderstandings follow and unfriendly accusations ar made before the surprise dénouement leaves Glenda covered wit embarrassment.

312 Little White Lies 3M 3F

Laura 'invents' a visit to a friend in Brighton to explain the unexpecte arrival at her parents' house. This arouses sister Muriel's suspicior regarding the Brighton conference husband Clive was to attend. I retaliation Laura and Clive stage a seduction scene which backfires wit the arrival of husband Alan. Another little white lie is revealed when transpires that Muriel and Alan had spent a night.... together? The pl thickens!

306 The Loved One 1M 2F

Lewis met Jane in Paris and romance briefly blossomed. Visiting her to renew the relationship he learns of Edward, her dead fiancé. A servant says he was engaged to the sister of whom Jane was insanely jealous and may have been responsible for the accident that killed them both. Lewis hastily retreats, leaving Jane fantasising of a Paris honeymoon with her loved one - Edward.

328 Season of Goodwill 3M 4F

Northerner Alfred, Works Foreman, has a new manager and neighbour, Humphrey, from the South. Amicable relations exist until Alfred's anticipated quiet Christmas without his mother-in-law. Humphrey's cockerel goes crowing berserk and in distraction Alfred does likewise. The rift escalates when Alfred vetoes the engagement of their respective offspring and finds himself isolated. Unexpected events conspire to heal the wounds but Alfred still has a problem.

239 Seeing Double 2M 3F

Attempting to end an affair, Quentin sends Lysette unknowingly to twin brother Justin for him to see her as Quentin with the latter liaising unseen through an internal intercom system. With Justin's wife mistaking Lysette as a new medical patient and Quentin's suspicious wife turning up the plan goes wrong causing "both brothers" to make ever-increasing frantic appearances in one guise or the other.

253 Two Sides of a Square 1M 3F

Maggie and Ernest share a successful relationship, each living alone on opposite sides of a town square. Ernest's carefree existence is shattered by Maggie's announcement that they should live together and start a family. Complications ensue with the intrusions of Nadine, Ernest's nubile new neighbour, and - across the square - the voyeur Miss Hebblewhite convinced that Ernest is a would-be rapist.